WOMEN OF THE STREETS

EARLY FRANCISCAN WOMEN
AND THEIR MENDICANT VOCATION

DARLEEN PRYDS

VOLUME SEVEN
THE FRANCISCAN HERITAGE SERIES

CFIT/ESC-OFM
2010

This booklet is the seventh in
The Franciscan Heritage Series
sponsored by the
Commission on the Franciscan Intellectual Tradition
of the English-speaking Conference of the
Order of Friars Minor
(CFIT/ESC-OFM)

General Editor
Joseph P. Chinnici, O.F.M.

Assistant Editor
Daria Mitchell, O.S.F.

ISBN: 1-57659-206-5
ISBN13: 978-1-57659-206-9

Library of Congress Control Number: 2010920134

Printed and bound in the United States of America
BookMasters, Inc.
Ashland, Ohio

TABLE OF CONTENTS

GENERAL EDITOR'S INTRODUCTION

Associate Professor of Christian Spirituality at the Franciscan School of Theology, Berkeley, Dr. Darleen Pryds is well known for her passionate commitment to a preached and lived Word supported by the best scholarship possible. In *Women of the Streets*, volume seven in the *Franciscan Heritage Series,* she admirably meets all of these goals in an engaging and thoughtful presentation of the lives and teaching of four significant medieval women who followed in the footsteps of Francis of Assisi. The Secretariat for the Retrieval of the Franciscan Intellectual Tradition is proud to sponsor her work. It is just this sort of presentation of the tradition which the Secretariat is trying to promote in its numerous publications, networking of scholars, website outreach, and mainstreaming of the insights of the tradition into the life of the ordinary believer.

With the publication of *Women of the Streets* Professor Pryds breaks new ground in the presentation of the Intellectual Tradition. Five previous volumes have concentrated on the theological and philosophical themes largely through the lenses of the academic reflections of Bonaventure and Scotus. One volume on the Gospel of John and the San Damiano Crucifix has opened up the field by interfacing the best of biblical theology with the icon of the crucified which spoke to Francis. Now Dr. Pryds argues for the tradition of "lived theology," what she calls "performative piety" or "somatic theology," through the examination of the lives and teachings of Rose of Viterbo, Angelo of Foligno, Margaret of Cortona, and Sancia, Queen of Naples. She correctly notes that these four women may serve as models for those who engage the intellectual tradition by living its central themes in the marketplace of life: an embrace of voluntary poverty, humility, compassionate outreach to others, public preaching, a personal embodiment of the love of the crucified Christ.

Long ago, Etienne Gilson pointed out that Bonaventure's work could be interpreted as the logical outcome of the lived theology of La Verna, its embodiment by Francis and its prayers of praise to God. Could it have been the lived tradition so well expressed in this present volume which also acted like a magnet on the academic tradition shaping its contours and focusing its central themes? We will never know for certain, but the relationships between the friars and the women studied here, the impact of their words and deeds on the populace, and the authenticity of a theology and spirituality which could express itself in such a startling mission in society and Church certainly bears testimony to the truth of an intellectual tradition that is meant to begin and end in Wisdom. There is a fundamental unity in the Franciscan tradition between thought and action, word and deed, theology and spirituality, the cell in which the indwelling Spirit lives and the marketplace of the world. The theology itself cannot be confined to the classroom, nor can it be understood outside of its lay practitioners, the men and women who have given it expression in the daily life of a changing society. Thanks to Dr. Pryds and her cohort of "women of the streets" we have a window into a significant dimension of an intellectual tradition rooted in a "light that descends to illumine our cognitive faculty, to bring joy to our affective power, and to strengthen our power of action." [Bonaventure, *Collations on the Seven Gifts of the Holy Spirit*, IX.5] We are most grateful.

At this time the Secretariat is also pleased to present its new website, franciscantradition.org which promises to extend the outreach of the Heritage volumes, the publications of the Washington Theological Union Symposium, and the numerous other intellectual activities supported most generously by the English Speaking Conference, Order of Friars

Minor. Further information may be found in the Introductions to the previous volumes in our Heritage Series.

Joseph P. Chinnici, O.F.M.
Franciscan School of Theology
Berkeley, California, 94709

PREFACE

This book is about women who pursued their life of faith in public. Specifically, this book explores the religious vocations that lay women adopted when they chose to become followers of Francis of Assisi in the first generations of the Franciscan movement. Rose of Viterbo, Angela of Foligno, Margaret of Cortona, and Sancia, Queen of Naples, were all born within the first century of the Franciscan Order. It is generally believed that women who followed a Franciscan call in these early years did so by joining Clare in her cloistered formulation of Franciscanism. But the women who are the focus of this book found their religious call outside monastic walls and pursued their vocations as laywomen in public and domestic spheres in late medieval Italian cities, that is, in the streets. Rather than taking up a monastic life in their response to their religious call, they followed Francis, and forged their lives as itinerant, lay, faithful women. As women who pursued their religious vocation of voluntary poverty, itinerancy, and preaching outside of monastic walls – in the streets and in their homes – they could very well be called the first generations of mendicant women.

Since the role of women within the Franciscan tradition has usually been studied with respect to Clare and her sisters who followed in Francis's footsteps primarily inside the cloister, a book about mendicant women outside the cloister is unique enough. But this short study goes further by positioning the texts about these early mendicant women within the history of the Franciscan intellectual tradition, a history usually written with respect to the theological, philosophical, and pastoral achievements of men. As we will see, women participated in the Franciscan life differently than men, so their participation within the intellectual tradition will necessarily be different. Some of these mendicant women did write texts themselves, and through these texts they impacted the spiritual journeys and religious lives of people around them. Other Franciscan laywomen wrote by dictating thoughts and ideas through male secretaries who probably altered and edited the women's words much like an editor or co-author today. And still other laywomen in this tradition spoke and taught in public, as well as in small domestic groups, which we might call faith-sharing groups. The words that these women used and the specific teachings they gave in their groups were never written down, so they have not been preserved, much like the words of catechists and many lay teachers within the Church today. Instead of their own words, we have accounts of their teaching moments which serve as important pieces of evidence of the religious leadership taken up by women following the Franciscan path in the thirteenth and fourteenth centuries.

The stories we have about these women teaching, debating, and preaching are as important to our understanding of the full range of the Franciscan intellectual tradition as are the sermons, commentaries, and treatises of Bonaventure, Scotus, or Ockham because these stories reveal how lay women gained a kind of religious education through their informal affiliations with the friars that in turn allowed them to attain significant roles of influence and leadership in their communities. These are stories within the Franciscan intellectual tradition that need to be told and retold today for a new generation of lay people choosing to follow Francis of Assisi, since most admirers of Francis today do not identify themselves as theologians, but as people of faith who admire the simple saint from Assisi.

To embrace a life of voluntary poverty has never been an easy choice – for men or women – nor has it ever been a popular one. These Franciscan women all had to struggle against peer pressure and at times clerical authority in order to persevere in their religious callings. Their personal struggle to persist in their dedication to their vocations is as much a part of their stories as are the other, more public displays of their Franciscan way of life. It is precisely because their personal and often private struggles to persevere as well as their inner determination can be overlooked in their stories that I emphasize them here. For just as today lay people face misunderstanding, bewilderment, and perhaps even ridicule from their peers for their acceptance of a counter-cultural way of life, these medieval Franciscan women faced friends, families, and powerful authorities, many of whom rebuked them, chastised them, scorned them, and shunned them because of the seriousness and depth of their religious call. In response, the Franciscan women of the thirteenth and early fourteenth centuries prayed, wept, doubted and, in the end, persevered in their religious vocations. If these women can be role models for lay Franciscans – both men and women – today, it can especially be in their perseverance in a counter-cultural embrace of voluntary poverty and life of faith.

The women discussed in this volume experienced their respective calls to the Franciscan way at various times in their lives: some had mid-life conversions; at least one gravitated to the friars and the Franciscan life from an early age, as a child, and took up a public apostolate by the age of ten; and still others seem to have had a life-long appreciation of the spiritual life, and increasingly dedicated their lives to their religious vocations. Some of these women were married and bore children; others were virgins. Some embraced a contemplative life away from the hustle and bustle of the city; others lived out their Franciscan vocation in the city streets. Some of these women quite literally preached to throngs of urban dwellers; others preached in private ways that were more in keeping with the traditional roles of medieval women. Regardless of their differences, they all looked to the historic image Francis of Assisi for their spiritual inspiration and sought to embody the Franciscan call in their own lives as women rather than in any theological texts they left behind. In this regard these women fit into the Franciscan intellectual tradition as somatic preachers and somatic theologians, that is, preachers and theologians living out theological precepts through their daily lives.[1]

While this book focuses on women and many women readers will be able to identify with the inner struggles and outer challenges of our cast, this book is not written just for female readers. I remember when I was a girl of twelve checking out a biography of Queen Elizabeth I from the library and the librarian told me, "This is a great girl-book." That phrase, "girl-book" stayed with me. Earlier that year I had checked out books about Lenin, Henry VIII, and the Beatles, but no librarian had ever commented on my reading selection until I checked out the biography of Elizabeth I. At that moment when the librarian told me I was checking out a "girl-book," I thought, "Why wouldn't boys read this book too? Why is it just a book for girls?"

This present book explores the issues and challenges of the interior spiritual and intellectual life that cross gender lines. The women in this volume chose to pursue and persevere in lives of faith against all odds. Such courage, determination, and resourcefulness offer inspiration and insights to both boys and girls; men and women. This is a book about women, and is intended for both men and women readers.

This volume is written as an introduction to the complex world of the first generations of lay Franciscan women. Care has been given to point to some of the most recent scholarship on each individual woman treated here, as well as to the Franciscan tradition as a whole, but even more attention has been given to presenting the stories of each woman so that readers can recognize reoccurring themes, challenges, and fruits of lay religious life from the late middle ages to today. The book is therefore intended for both an introductory academic audience and a general audience interested in studying role models of lay religious for personal and spiritual reflection.

---

[1] I am presently completing two studies on this somatic practice among lay Franciscan women "Lay Franciscan Women and the Practice of Somatic Preaching," forthcoming in *Franciscan Preaching*, ed. Timothy Johnson (Leiden: Brill, in preparation); "Angela of Foligno as a Somatic Theologian," forthcoming in a Festschrift for William J. Courtenay.

To facilitate this multi-folded use, each section follows the same organization: 1) a narrative account of the woman's story; 2) an analytical discussion of themes for consideration; 3) two series of questions: one for general discussion and one for spiritual reflection.

Writing this book would have been a much lonelier enterprise without the lively conversation, help and companionship of many people. I would especially like to thank Scott Graham, who patiently accepts my extended mental forays into the medieval past. For this I am grateful. The ever-changing community of the Franciscan School of Theology in Berkeley, which is part of the larger ever-changing community of the Graduate Theological Union, nurtured this book into being more than any one of them will ever know. Among the people who offered insights, suggestions, and concrete help are Joseph Chinnici, Mary Ann Donovan, Lisa Fullam, Lezlie Knox, Marian Mollin, Joanne Parrilli, Daniel Joslyn-Siemiakoski, and Rebecca Lyman. Ideas that fed into this book were also tried out on various audiences at the International Medieval Congress at Kalamazoo; the Franciscan Retreat Center in Scottsdale, Arizona; the Summer Preaching Institute at Aquinas Institute in St. Louis (2005 and 2008); the 10th Annual Franciscan Symposium, "Franciscan Evangelization: Striving to Preach the Gospel" sponsored by the Franciscan Center of the Washington Theological Union; my classes, at FST/GTU, especially my History of Women and Religious Leadership class; and the Franciscan Vision series sponsored by the Franciscan School of Theology. Any errors of fact or interpretation that remain are mine alone.

Special thanks go to Joe Chinnici, O.F.M. for usually demonstrating the patience of a saint.

CHAPTER ONE

WOMEN AND THE MENDICANT TRADITION

What do the following women have in common: a willful teenage girl; a married woman in the midst of a mid-life crisis; an unmarried woman, who was left alone and socially alienated after the death of her long-time live-in lover; and a prayerful queen who shunned her "duty" to bear children? They were all laywomen who embraced a religious quest by imitating the life of Francis of Assisi in the first few generations after the saint's death in 1226. By following the Franciscan vocation of poverty and itinerancy, these laywomen transgressed their respective social and cultural positions, especially with regard to their gender. Rose of Viterbo (d. 1251), Angela of Foligno (d. 1309), Margaret of Cortona (d. 1297), and Sancia of Naples (d. 1352) stand out among the lay Franciscan women of their time having gained fame for their lifestyles. But how many people have heard about them today? Despite their respective fame among their medieval contemporaries, why have their stories of religious conviction and perseverance been generally neglected and remain largely unknown?

Part of the answer to this question lies in the fact that these women pursued their religious calling within the broader mendicant movement, that is the movement that grew out of the twelfth century tradition of itinerancy, preaching, and voluntary poverty as a way of life.[2] Since the beginning of mendicancy as a religious calling, this form of vocation has been deemed daring and admirable for men, but inappropriate for women. While the religious vocation of Francis of Assisi captured the imagination of thousands of men who left their families and followed his lead to become a mendicant friar in the early thirteenth century, women who were similarly moved by Francis's dedication to apostolic poverty and who experienced the same desire to follow in his footsteps were usually hindered by social, legal, and moral rules forbidding women to live an unsheltered and unprotected life. When women felt a similar call to mendicancy, the choice presented to them looked very different from Francis's own life of itinerant preaching and intense periods of solitary contemplation. For most early Franciscan women, the desire to follow in Francis's footsteps as a wandering preacher and beggar led them by cultural default to accept a vocation to follow in Clare's footsteps into the enclosed world of the convent. Many of these women who were inspired by Francis or by the friars, no doubt, found a satisfying spiritual home within the cloistered walls. But, some women forged ahead and embraced mendicant life not as nuns in habits inside monasteries, but as laywomen in urban streets and homes. These women followed their Franciscan call by embracing poverty, by offering works of charity to their peers, and by preaching and teaching. This book gives a brief introduction to their stories by exploring how four different women took to the streets to live out their religious vocations by embodying Franciscan ideals.[3] These

---

[2] The best introduction to this movement remains Herbert Grundmann, *Religious Movements in the Middle Ages*, tran. Steven Rowan (Notre Dame: University of Notre Dame Press, 1995).

[3] Shorter versions of material found in this book are found in my articles, "Following Francis: Laywomen and the Scandalous Call to be Franciscan," *Listening* 41.2 (2006): 85-95; and "Preaching Women: The Tradition of Mendicant Women" in *Franciscan Evangelization: Striving to Preach the Gospel,* Washington Theological Union Symposium Papers 7 (St. Bonaventure, NY: Franciscan Institute Publications, 2008), 55-77.

women, then, can be seen to represent the embodied theology of the lay Franciscan movement.

CHARISMATIC WOMEN FOLLOWING A CHARISMATIC PATH

Today notions of the Franciscan tradition often zero in on the individual charismatic founder of the movement, Francis of Assisi. Images of Francis commonly emphasize a gentle man talking to birds or an impassioned youth renouncing parental control by stripping off his clothes in the town square as a bold statement of his religious vocation. His charismatic expressions of faith still appeal to us today, so that it is not difficult for us to imagine how he would have attracted the attention of his contemporaries.[4] By the time Francis died in 1226, his followers had grown in numbers to such an extent that it was easy to identify the existence of an established order of friars.[5]

While Francis was certainly charismatic, and the success his order experienced in recruiting new members can in large part be attributed to his personal magnetism, it would be inaccurate to assume that what Francis and his followers did had been unique or unprecedented. Contemporary admirers found in the growing band of friars a group that modeled the religious idealism of the day: the *vita apostolica*, or the apostolic life. The *vita apostolica* was more than a mere fad, but it would be an overstatement to call it an actual "movement," if one were to mean by that an organization of adherents

---

[4] A brief introduction to Francis and his influence through the centuries can be found in William J. Short, *Poverty and Joy. The Franciscan Tradition* (Maryknoll, NY: Orbis, 1999).

[5] For an overview of the beginnings and growth of the nascent Franciscan Order, see Grado Merlo, *In the Name of Saint Francis. History of the Friars Minor and Franciscanism until the 16th Century*, tran. Raphael Bonanno, ed. Robert Karris (St. Bonaventure, NY: Franciscan Institute Publications, 2009); and Maurice Carmody, *The Franciscan Story. St. Francis of Assisi and His Influence since the 13th Century* (London: Athena Press, 2008).

following some coherently articulated agenda. If one were to have in mind something as nebulous and as broad as "the peace movement" of the 1960s in the United States, one could imagine the same kind of movement made up of various local groups with a broad appeal and general adherence to similar aspirations and ideals, but with no formal or even loose organization. In the case of the *vita apostolica*, the shared ideal was based on defining and living the Christian life as one in direct imitation of Jesus and his original apostles especially with regard to poverty and itinerancy.[6] Such a life implied a religious vocation that was lived out in the streets in public without any of the institutional trappings and political complexities of the contemporary Church. The friars were public figures, and embodied this new model of religious life – one that was in and part of the world, not separated from the world by a monastery wall.

The very public nature of the friars' vocation raised immediate problems for women wishing to participate in this new form of religious life. The social norms for thirteenth century western European women allowed for some public roles for women, especially for middle class women in cities where their increasing participation in growing urban businesses was rather common. But public speech and itinerant travel, both of which were part of the friars' life, were unbecoming and usually forbidden to women of any class or social rank.[7] Women who dared to speak in public, even when their speech was religious or pious discourse, were generally assumed to be promiscuous.[8]

---

[6] See Grundmann, *Religious Movements in the Middle Ages*.

[7] A good introduction to the role of women in the Middle Ages is found in the essays in P. Ariès and G. Duby, eds. *A History of Private Life*, Vol. 2, *Revelations of the Medieval World*, tran. A. Goldhammer, (Cambridge, MA: Belknap Press, 1988).

[8] In the twelfth century there were on-going rhetorical attacks on female preachers as promiscuous; see Beverly Mayne Kienzle, "The Prostitute-Preacher: Patterns of Polemic against Medieval Waldensian Women Preachers," in B.M. Kienzle and P. Walker, eds. *Women Preachers and Prophets through Two Millennia of Christianity* (Berkeley: University of California Press, 1998), 99-113. For the continued struggle of women in the twelfth and thirteenth century to find opportunities to speak in public, see

How, then, could devout, faith-filled women adopt the Franciscan life as their own? Traditionally, scholars have answered this question by looking immediately to Clare and her order. Clare, it has been understood, offered the feminine form of the Franciscan life, since she, herself, had been the first woman to try to follow Francis. When she fled from her family on Palm Sunday in 1212, she made her own religious commitment in front of Francis, who cut her hair and invested her with clothes of poverty.[9] Clare embraced her own mendicant call and adapted it to a cloistered model of religious vocation.[10] She initially took up residence in a series of Benedictine convents, until she and her own small group of followers could settle at San Damiano, just outside the Assisi, where they developed a form of the Franciscan life within monastic walls.

Traditionally this monasticizing of Clare and her vocation has been interpreted by scholars as the necessary act of recourse required to secure Clare's safety and to insure the reputation of the friars. Given medieval mores on gender relations, Clare's presence within Francis's circle of followers would have caused scandal for the friars and would have created a risky, or even perilous, situation for Clare.[11] More recently, scholars have endeavored to show Clare's

---

Jo Ann McNamara, "The Rhetoric of Orthodoxy: Clerical Authority and Female Innovation in the Struggle with Heresy," in *Maps of Flesh and Light. The Religious Experience of Medieval Women Mystics*, ed. Ulrike Wiethaus, (Syracuse: Syracuse University Press, 1993), 9-27.

[9] For a discussion of the complexities of this scene, see Margaret Carney, *The First Franciscan Woman: Clare of Assisi and Her Form of Life* (Quincy: Franciscan Press, 1993), 36-39.

[10] The research on Clare and the development of her order has become rich in the last 25 years; see especially Carney, *The First Franciscan Woman;* Ingrid Peterson, *Clare of Assisi* (Quincy: Franciscan Press, 1993); Catherine Mooney, "*Imitatio Christi* or *Imitatio Mariae*? Clare of Assisi and Her Interpreters," in *Gendered Voices. Medieval Saints and Their Interpreters*, ed. Catherine Mooney, (Philadelphia: University of Pennsylvania Press, 1999), 52-77; and Lezlie Knox, *Creating Clare of Assisi. Female Franciscan Identities in Late Medieval Italy* (Leiden: Brill, 2008).

[11] For example see Christiane Klapisch-Zuber, ed., *A History of Women in the West*. Vol. 2 *Silences of the Middle Ages* (Cambridge, MA: Belknap Press, 1992), 314.

self-determination in her vocational choices.[12] Regardless of the contextual interpretation one accepts, it remains true that Clare's life as a Franciscan was a life lived out primarily within monastic walls as a cloistered sister with timely, dramatic forays outside. As Margaret Carney summarizes, "[Clare] dared to synthesize the evangelical ideals of Francis, the new forms of urban female religiosity, and the best wisdom of the monastic tradition to create a new and enduring order in the Church."[13]

This monastic form of the feminine expression of the Franciscan charism was not the only way women followed in Francis's steps, however. In fact, many women were inspired by stories heard about Francis, and thereby sought to follow in his footsteps outside a monastic compound by remaining in their own homes. Both men and women felt called by this lay form of religious vocation, and adopted a Franciscan way of life by remaining with their families in their homes as lay Franciscans who were called "penitentials" by contemporaries.[14] This lay movement was not directly founded by Francis nor did it begin as an officially sanctioned lay alternative to his form of vowed religious life. But as the Franciscan movement expanded, the friars indirectly inspired without actively promoting, the growth of the lay penitential movement. The women discussed here in this book are part of this larger lay penitential movement that included men.

---

[12] The emphasis on Clare's self-determination is found especially among scholars within the Franciscan family; see Carney, *The First Franciscan Woman*; and Peterson, *Clare of Assisi*, for example.

[13] Carney, *The First Franciscan Woman*, 19.

[14] On the forms of religious life chosen by women at this time, see Mario Sensi, "Anchoresses and Penitents in Thirteenth and Fourteenth-Century Umbria," in D. Bornstein and R Rusconi, eds., *Women and Religion in Medieval and Renaissance Italy* (Chicago: University of Chicago Press, 1996), 56-83.

GROUNDBREAKING PRECEDENT:
THE *VITA APOSTOLICA* AND THE RISE OF MENDICANCY

While there are original aspects to Francis and the order he founded, his dedication to the apostolic life, especially with regard to embracing poverty and taking up an itinerant life were not unprecedented. In the century prior to Francis's conversion around 1206, there are several documented cases of other middle class and aristocratic men who had abandoned the material comforts of their lives to take up a form of religious life not confined by monastic walls. The most famous of these was Peter Waldo, the founder of the group known as the Waldensians. The *vita apostolica*, or "apostolic life movement" of the twelfth century developed just as people were moving to cities within Western Europe and long distance trade was contributing to economic prosperity. Along with these economic developments came higher literacy rates among western Europeans, which contributed to an overall flourishing of a cosmopolitan flair to the region.[15] In part a spiritual response to this growing prosperity, and in part a widespread call for religious reform, the *vita apostolica* attracted lay people who tried as best they could to imitate the lives of the apostles. They eagerly sought out Scripture that could be read in the vernacular, and met in groups to talk about faith and to learn more about the lives of the original followers of Christ. They placed secondary importance on material wealth and instead followed a counter-cultural path of material simplicity. Because they sought a life of penance, they were known as "Penitents" and their groups were called "Penitentials."[16]

---

[15] See H. Grundmann, *Religious Movements*; G.G. Meersseman, *Dossier de l'ordre de la Pénitence au XIIIe siècle* (Fribourg: Editions universitaires, 1961).

[16] In addition to the works in the preceding note, see André Vauchez, "Medieval Penitents," in *The Laity in the Middle Ages. Religious Beliefs and Devotional Practices*, ed. Daniel Bornstein, tran. Margery Schneider (Notre Dame: University of Notre Dame Press, 1993), 119-27.

The eventual creation of a Third Order, or an order of lay affiliates to the Franciscan Order, grew out of this preceding penitential movement during the thirteenth century, albeit with some reticence on the part of the friars. The important precedent to note is the prior existence of the Penitentials. In fact one could claim that it was the penitential movement that had originally inspired Francis himself, and that it was his creation of a modified, vowed form of the penitential life that became the order of Friars Minor that eventually furthered the lay movement and ultimately led to its regularization with institutional structures and requirements.[17]

Not surprising, then, ever since the time of Francis, himself, there were some women who were attracted to his way of religious life and sought ways to adopt the mendicant life for themselves, either as "freelance" female mendicants or, more commonly, by affiliating with the friars as "hangers-on." But it was precisely this affiliation with the friars that caused tensions and problems. Francis had been reticent to accept women followers, as is evidenced by his preference for Clare to create a cloistered form of life for women. While Francis may have appreciated the religious fervor of his lay followers – both men and women – he never demonstrated interest in promoting any official affiliation of lay people to his order.[18]

Some friars who followed Francis proved to be colder to and even more wary of lay affiliation. An anonymous author

---

[17] André Vauchez and Joanna Cannon, *Margherita of Cortona and the Lorenzetti. Sienese Art and the Cult of a Holy Woman in Medieval Tuscany* (University Park: Pennsylvania State University Press, 1999), 18, argue similarly, at least in terms of Francis and his movement furthering the penitential movement. They stop short of arguing that the penitential movement actually inspired Francis. On the penitential movements of twelfth and thirteenth century Italy, see A. Vauchez, "Pénitents au Moyen Age," *Dictionnaire de Spiritualité*, XII, (Paris, 1984), cols. 1010-1023; and G. Meersseman, *Ordo Fraternitatis: Confraternite e pietà dei laici nel Medioevo*, Italia Sacra, vols. 24-26 (Rome: Herder, 1977).

[18] On the friars and the penitents, or lay mendicants, see B. Schlager, "Foundress of the Franciscan Life: Umiliana Cerchi and Margaret of Cortona," *Viator* 29 (1998): 141-66 at 154-57. More specifically, on the friars and lay women, see Brenda Bolton, *"Mulieres Sanctae,"* in *Sanctity and Secularity: The Church and the World,* ed. Derek Baker, Studies in Church History 10 (Oxford: Blackwell, 1973), 87-91.

from the late thirteenth century made the case against lay affiliation in an academic treatise entitled, "Why the Brothers Should not Promote the Order of Penitents."[19] High on the list of reasons not to get involved with lay people in general but especially with laywomen, was the belief that the friars would lose their freedom if there were an official relationship developed with laity and the Order. The friars could become embroiled in legal disputes involving lay affiliates that could have financial or material repercussions. The author was especially wary of friars involving themselves with women. For example, if a laywoman who affiliated with the friars were to become pregnant or were to raise suspicion and gossip for licentious behavior, the friars would immediately be suspected as guilty of the same crimes because of her affiliation to the order. The risk of such scandal and the resulting distractions from their true vocations were reason enough for avoiding association with any laywoman, according to the author. Interestingly, the author does not expand on the potential for sexual misconduct among the friars themselves, but instead rests his focus of the potential for temptation on laywomen.

The anonymous author further argues that if friars were to meet regularly with lay affiliates, for example in prayer groups or what we might today call faith-sharing groups, they would run the serious risk of being charged with heresy if they were to meet in private. Earlier followers of the *vita apostolica* in the twelfth century, such as the Waldensians, had faced heresy charges after they had met in private for spiritual and religious purposes.[20] The assumption that independent lay people were inclined toward heresy was still

---

[19] The treatise was associated with Bonaventure and appears in an edition of the great Franciscan's Complete Works as *Determinationes quaestionum circa regulam Fratrum Minorum*, pt. 2, q. 16 in *Bonaventurae Opera Omnia* 8 (Quaracchi: Collegium S. Bonaventurae, 1898), 368-69. This work will be quoted as Pseudo-Bonaventure with page number.

[20] On the association of Waldensians with heresy, see Euan Cameron, *Waldenses: Rejections of Holy Church in Medieval Europe* (Oxford: Blackwell, 2000); R.I. Moore, *The Formation of a Persecuting Society: Power and Deviance in Western Europe, 950-1250* (Oxford: Blackwell, 1987, 2nd ed., 2007).

widespread in the late thirteenth century. For this reason, the friar-author thought it would be prudent for his order to avoid close affiliations with laity, faithful though they may be.

And finally, the role of laity within the order could not be regulated, the anonymous author argues. While friars took vows of obedience, lay affiliates would not be bound in obedience to the Franciscans. Therefore their behavior at work and at home could not be monitored, nor could any code of behavior be enforced upon them by the friars. The author presumes that the risk of temptations in the world and of the flesh would press on the lay affiliate and the friars would have no control. The affiliates' behavior would naturally reflect on the friars, who could not be expected to risk the potential for such scandal. "Indeed, wouldn't discipline and justice dissolve under our own hands?" he poignantly asks.[21]

Therefore, in order to control the vocational focus of the friars and to protect them from the risk of public scandal resulting from possible bad behavior of lay affiliates, the friar took a position concerning lay affiliates that the order often tried to take: one that was wary of official connections to lay people, especially to women.

Given this Franciscan's circumspection concerning lay people – especially lay women – it would be easy to assume that all friars kept a distance from the laity. But in fact this institutional stance of distancing the friars from the laity coexisted with the reality of periodic close relationships and rapport between friars and individual lay people, including lay women.[22] The friars were, after all, called to pastoral ministry. In this capacity they often functioned as confessors to lay people. This relationship could develop into one of ongoing conversation that we would call spiritual direction, to-

---

[21] See Pseudo Bonaventure, 369: "... *quin cito dilaberetur sub manibus nostris disciplina et iusticia?*"

[22] For a brief overview of the rapport that developed between the friars and lay women, see Anna Benvenuti Papi, "Mendicant Friars and Female Pinzochere in Tuscany: From Social Marginality to Models of Sanctity," in *Women and Religion in Medieval and Renaissance Italy*, D. Bornstein and R. Rusconi, eds. (Chicago: University of Chicago Press, 1996), 84-103.

day. As is often the case in spiritual direction, there can be a mutuality of sharing truths of faith and pieces of wisdom, so that the directee influences the director just as the director influences the directee. It is clear that the same thing happened at times among friars who were confessors to lay women in the thirteenth and fourteenth centuries. The growth of mutual respect and mutual influence was such that at times the laywomen seemed to be the spiritual teacher.[23] We can find this kind of relationship developed for Rose of Viterbo, Angela of Foligno, Margaret of Cortona, and Sancia of Naples with their respective confessors, so we know that while there was an institutional wariness of friars developing close relationships with lay women, the reality was different. It was through these close relationships that did develop between friars and laywomen that the intellectual underpinnings of the Franciscan way of life were spread and translated into a lay form that was then lived out in the lives of women. The intellectual tradition of the order was adopted by laywomen and thus spread more deeply into their contemporary society and culture as these women modeled Franciscan tenets of faith in their everyday lives. It was through their everyday lives that these women cultivated and spread the Franciscan way of life in a way that could be called a form of lay preaching.

Preaching as a Mendicant Charism

Preaching was a central tenet of all the mendicant movements from their beginning, but especially for the Dominicans

---

[23] On the influence of laywomen on their confessors see John Coakley, "Friars as Confidants of Holy Women in Medieval Dominican Hagiography," in *Images of Sainthood in Medieval Europe*, R. Blumenfeld-Kosinski and T. Szell, eds. (Ithaca: Cornell University Press, 1991), 222-46. While Coakley specifically analyzes the confessor/confessee relationship among Dominicans, the same rapport can be found among Franciscans. Also see Coakley's study, *Women, Men, and Spiritual Power. Female Saints and their Male Collaborators* (New York: Columbia University Press, 2006).

and the Franciscans. It is commonly believed that women could only marginally participate in these movements since women were not allowed to preach. Within the Christian tradition as far back as Paul there are often-quoted proscriptions about women and public speech. "Let a woman learn in silence with full submission. I permit no woman to teach or to have authority over a man; she is to keep silent" (1 Tim. 2:11-12). Conciliar decisions from the early Church had used Pauline proscriptions as precedent and justification to expect silence from Christian women: "Even a woman who is learned and holy should not presume to teach men in a public assembly."[24]

These expectations of female silence were resurrected and repeated in the thirteenth century. A thirteenth century anonymous, presumably male author, compiling a code of behavior for female recluses specified to the women:

> Do not preach to anyone.... St. Paul forbade women to preach.... Do not criticize any man, nor blame him for his vices unless he is over-familiar with you. Holy old anchoresses may do it in a certain way, but it is not a sure thing, nor is it proper for the young. It is the business of those who are set over others and have to guard them, as teachers of holy Church.[25]

But there is a funny thing about legal proscriptions. They are issued when the behavior they prohibit is occurring. Such is the case with lay preaching, and especially with women's preaching in the twelfth and thirteenth centuries. Women and laymen were taking to the street to proclaim the Gospel as part of their embrace of the *vita apostolica*. And there in the streets and city squares, they issued forth with a kind

---

[24] For an overview of proscriptions against women's public speech, see my article, "Proclaiming Sanctity through Proscribed Acts: The Case of Rose of Viterbo," in *Women Preachers and Prophets*, B. Kienzle and P. Walker, eds., 159-72 esp. 159-62.

[25] *Ancrene Wisse*, based on a translation by A. Savage and N. Watson (New York: Paulist Press), 75.

of preaching that was informal and non-doctrinal. In keeping with the guidelines about lay preaching delineated in a preaching handbook by Thomas Chobham writing in the 1230s, the licit lay preachers of the time did not preach in a church, and certainly did not preach within a liturgical context. Similarly, they did not presume to preach on issues directly related to doctrine that would require special theological education, nor did they expound on Scripture *per se*, which would also require advanced education. Instead, lay preachers "commended virtues and renounced vices" outside of a church. Lay preachers never received a formal preaching license, but they were required to receive the permission of local clergy.[26] Therefore, rather than being universally and comprehensively banned and prohibited, lay preaching could and did exist with clerical approval and support in many parts of medieval Europe.

While never common and always under some veil of either concern or flat out suspicion, there clearly was a window of opportunity for women to be street preachers in the twelfth-fifteenth centuries. In this capacity, women (and lay men) may have exhorted people, commended virtues, encouraged people in their faith, and offered words of praise to Christ in the streets and piazzas of medieval Italy, and just like their clerical counterparts, these street preachers would have attracted admiration from some and critical disdain from others. But as long as these preachers – whether lay or clerical – were not presuming to preach doctrinal issues or expound Holy Scripture in Church, and as long as they received at least tacit approval from local church officials, a fair amount of street preaching occurred, and it appears that some women took part. We will see that Rose of Viterbo took to the streets and shouted words of encouragement to the citizens of Viterbo to attend church. And both Angela of Foligno and Margaret of Cortona made striking statements about personal penance when they processed through the

---

[26] Thomas de Chobham, *Summa de arte praedicandi*, ed. Franco Morenzoni, Corpus Christianorum, Cont. Med., vol. 82 (Turnhout: Brepols, 1988), 57.

streets of their respective cities in a kind of theatrical performance that could very well be labeled a kind of preaching.
Each of these Franciscan lay women received some criticism
from family and friends for the public spectacles they made
of their faith but this criticism is no different from the kind of
public ridicule and attention many clerical itinerant preachers received at the same time. Just like today, street preaching was a tough business, not for the faint-hearted. The fact
that these women took to the streets and preached in the face
of criticism and derision points to the depth of their faith and
the thickness of their skin. Franciscan laywomen were not
quiet and demure. They were outspoken and strong-willed.
Perhaps this is one reason their stories were suppressed for
so long.

EXCEPTIONAL WOMEN, ORDINARY LIVES

While all of the Franciscan women in this volume are laywomen, none of them was an ordinary laywoman, if such a
person ever exists. So we must ask to what extent the lives of
these exceptional women can tell us anything about the average lives of people in the early lay Franciscan movement.
Each one of the women studied here stood out among her
contemporaries either for her local leadership in religious
and spiritual affairs, her special reputation for holiness, or
her social rank and office. Yet, the vast majority of the early
lay Franciscans – both men and women – remain nameless
and unknown to us these 800 years later, since their lives
were considered ordinary, not warranting particular mention
or documentation. On the one hand, the lack of documentation for the vast majority of devout lay people following a
Franciscan path in the thirteenth and fourteenth centuries
tells us that the movement had attained a certain level of
public credibility and acceptability. The way of life had become so readily accepted, it no longer warranted note in any
official documentation or contemporary chronicle. But, this

also means that learning the details of their lives of devotion and how these lay Franciscans incorporated their serious devotional lives into their lives that included family and work-related responsibilities is thus impossible. We are left with an historical situation for which we must look at the documentation that does exist for us to get some glimpse at the lay Franciscan movement in general. For this we have information about those women who for some reasons stood out among their peers. To ask the reader to accept these exceptional women as representative of lay Franciscan lives may be a stretch. But historians are bound by the problem of sources. We can explore the past only by way of the historical sources. Much like our newspapers today relate stories of unusual and exceptional people and events – those things that are considered "newsworthy" – historical sources of all kinds or genres document that which was considered worth the cost and effort to write down on parchment. That usually means news about exceptional people.

In the cases of the Franciscan women in this volume, the genres of sources that are available for studying their lives include hagiography, spiritual autobiography, personal letters, official papal and royal letters. Each of these kinds of sources has its own particular uses and interpretive dangers for us when we are trying to draw the lives and piety of laywomen, but probably the trickiest for modern students to use is hagiography. Since all the women presented here in this study were at one point or another considered a candidate for canonization, at least briefly, the particular challenges of hagiography as a source needs to be addressed, so that we are not overly gullible when relying on these sources, nor are we cynically dismissive.

Hagiography or saints' lives are literary pieces crafted with the special intent to cultivate and inspire the widespread belief that someone was a holy person. In some cases hagiography also has the added agenda to promote a would-be saint as someone worthy of official canonization.[27] That

---

[27] The best treatments of medieval saint-making are André Vauchez, *Sainthood in the Later Middle Ages*, tran. Jean Birrell, (Cambridge: Cam-

is, they are pieces of literature written with a clear political and social agenda: to publicize and promote the cult or belief of a saint. The author of hagiography sets out on a different task from the author of biography in that the former molds the biographical facts of a person into generally accepted and recognizable characteristics of sanctity. Someone who is not recognized by their contemporaries as a holy person will not be known or revered as a saint. Therefore, hagiography tends to be rather formulaic in its depictions.

When there are shifts in expectations of holiness in history in any given society, these changes appear in that society's hagiography. The thirteenth century saw just such a shift take place to fit the new urban society of Western Europe with the quick canonization of Francis in 1228, just two years after his death in 1226. With the general and ready acceptance of Francis as a holy man, and then with the official recognition of him as a canonized saint, Christian Europe saw a new model of holiness: an itinerant beggar and preacher who embraced the apostolic life rather than a monastic life of prayerful stability. Within a generation or two of Francis's canonization, there began to be cases brought to the Roman curia of lay women, such as Rose of Viterbo and, a little later, Margaret of Cortona, who, like Francis, walked the path to holiness by way of poverty, preaching, and itinerancy. Biographical fact? We may never know. What is more compelling is to notice that such cases exist and such hagiography was written with laywomen as its protagonist, since the existence of this hagiography reveals the contemporary society's desire and recognition of such women as holy. The fact that Rose of Viterbo in the mid-thirteenth century could be seen as holy, while women just fifty to eighty years earlier who preached the Word were denounced as prostitutes

---

bridge University Press, 1997); and Guy Philippart, ed., *Hagiographies. Histoire internationale de la littérature hagiographique latine et ver- naculaire en Occident des origines à 1550,* Vols. 1-3 (Turnhout: Brepols, 1994-2001). A good, succinct discussion of hagiography is found in R.C. Van Caenegem, *Guide to the Sources of Medieval History,* Europe in the Middle Ages. Selected Studies, Vol. 2 (Amsterdam: North-Holland Publishing, 1978), 50-54.

points to a significant shift in social expectations of holiness and society's reception of certain behavior as saintly.[28] The popular allure of the Franciscan charism in general largely explains this shift in medieval expectations of holiness. This book points to how women participated in these new public and urban standards of holiness, and suggests that such a model of holiness is appropriate to reinstate today.

Other sources used in this study include spiritual autobiography which one could readily term autohagiography. The *Memorial* of Angela of Foligno is just such a source. Much like hagiography, this kind of source needs to be read with a critical eye, but the same richness for discovering the history of women is found here.

And finally, these women's stories are told through their letters – both personal letters and official papal or royal letters. Of the women discussed here, Angela of Foligno and Sancia of Naples both wrote letters that conveyed spiritual or political interpretations of the Franciscan life. None of their letters, though, should be viewed as revealing the inner, most intimate desires of their author. All letters from the period were assumed to be public. Privacy was rare. So again, these sources are public, intended to circulate for public consumption. Therefore, they reflect a kind of propaganda or spin of any situation or biographical detail.[29] Nevertheless, we can see how early Franciscan women positioned themselves vis-à-vis individual friars or the entire order, and how they saw themselves as protectors of the Franciscan way of life. These women were not passive admirers of Francis or the friars; they actively carved out for themselves leadership roles to interpret how the Franciscan charism should be lived, and to cultivate and safeguard opportunities for their preferred way. Letters had the capacity to express both spiritual and political authority, and some early Franciscan women, name-

---

[28] B. Kienzle, "The Prostitute Preacher," in *Women Preachers and Prophets*, ed. B. Kienzle and P. Walker, 99-113.

[29] On letters as a historical source, see R.C. Van Caenegem, *Guide to the Sources of Medieval History*, 55-57; and Giles Constable, *Letters and Letter Collections* (Turnhout: Brepols, 1976).

ly Angela of Foligno and Sancia of Naples, used their pens to deliver just such authority.

Rose of Viterbo, Angela of Foligno, Margaret of Cortona, and Sancia of Naples could not have been more different in biographical detail. Their ages ranged from child and adolescent to mature old-age. They lived in disparate stations of life, ranging from disenfranchised poverty to royalty. Nevertheless, their lives as lay Franciscan women bear some resemblance. The features they hold in common include the following:

1. Each woman discussed in this volume participated in and contributed to the intellectual tradition of the Franciscan movement primarily through their embodied spirituality. None of these women were formally educated in Franciscan *studia* in the friars' intellectual tradition like their male counterparts. Instead, these women learned Franciscan theology and spirituality informally from confessors and preachers; they cultivated their understanding of Franciscan beliefs by adopting the precepts within the contexts of their respective lives; and they viscerally experienced the fundamental precepts of the tradition, especially with regard to poverty, humility, and devotion to the passion of Christ. From living out these precepts, the women studied here went on to share their understanding of the Franciscan tradition in their words and deeds. Their participation in the Franciscan intellectual tradition is necessarily different from their male counterparts, and deserves to be recognized in its rightful place within this tradition on its own terms.

2. These women all modeled their spiritual lives on Francis himself rather than Clare. Clare may figure in some of their lives as an inspiration and some of them may try to become Poor Clare sisters, but in their initial and fundamental call to religious life, they were influenced by Francis and sought to follow in his footsteps. None of these women knew Francis directly or personally, so they cultivated their vocation based on images they had

of him whether that be from stories told by friars, artistic representations, or preaching.

3. They all exhibited a performative piety, that is, a religious devotion that was physically expressive. This performative piety was very much in keeping with their urban and public call to mendicancy. Theirs was not a private religious devotion, cultivated alone in a cell. Although each of them may at times have found inspiration in periods of solitary contemplation, just as Francis had, their call to religious life – their call to the Franciscan life – compelled each of them to perform their faith in public.

4. As a result of their performative piety, they often suffered detractors and brought to themselves public (and private) ridicule because of how they expressed their faith. The public performances of their religious devotion were especially considered shocking to their peers, so that their very religious call as Franciscan women was a public scandal.

5. Each one persevered in their call to be a mendicant woman, despite this local criticism, which at times came from the friars themselves. Each of these lay Franciscan women cultivated inner resources that allowed them to overcome conflict and to resolve differences of opinion.

6. Each one had to adapt to challenges and constantly reform and craft their lives in response to changes and challenges. In this regard, they each showed a flexibility in their vocation and more generally in their lives.[30]

7. Each woman experienced a profound piety that was grounded in identifying with the suffering Christ. This identification with the passion of Christ was not an end in and of itself. Instead it led to the cultivation of compassion for others, and thus lay at the heart of Franciscan theology.

For all of these reasons, these lay Franciscan women are important to consider and study in order to understand the

---

[30] This flexibility in life choices is one shared by many women today; see Mary Catherine Bateson, *Composing a Life* (New York: Plume, 1989).

full expression of the Franciscan intellectual tradition. As representatives of lay Franciscans, they may be seen in some regards as precursors and even models today to lay people who seek to follow in the footsteps of Francis. More important than any writings they penned and left behind, the stories of their lives demonstrate the influence these women had among their contemporaries through their embodiment of Franciscan theology. Their place in the intellectual tradition of the Franciscans is strikingly different from that of the philosophers and theologians who appear in other volumes of this series. Instead of formally writing, debating, or preaching Franciscan theology, these women experienced and shared Franciscan theology through their lives. Thus, it is to their life stories we turn in order to understand the role of women in the Franciscan intellectual tradition.

CHAPTER TWO

ROSE OF VITERBO (D. 1251)
A FRANCISCAN STREET PREACHER

Rose of Viterbo was born around 1233 just a few years after Francis of Assisi died in 1226. Already by the time Rose was born, Francis's influence was gaining a hold in Viterbo, the central Italian city where Rose lived. Friars established a church there by 1236 and were making a significant impression on the citizens. The Franciscans especially captured the imagination of one little girl named Rose, who imitated the friars by dressing up in a copy of their habit, insisting on having her hair shaved into the tonsure of a cleric, and begging her mother to secure for her thick rope to tie around her habit like the Franciscans did. But Rose's pious dress-up was not something she just played at home. Clad in a habit tied by the cord, Rose took to the streets and played the part of a friar by preaching. When Rose brought her pious followers back home to continue her spiritual teaching there, her parents objected. They tried to stifle their daughter's passionate expressions of faith, but to no avail. Rose's unselfconscious imitation of the friars captured the attention and imagination of her contemporaries and positioned her as someone who challenged social expectations of proper comportment for a girl and a young woman. But it was the audacious manner in which she used her imitation of the friars to voice opposition to Emperor Frederick II, the arch-enemy of the pope at the time, that raised the ante on the extent to which the girl would break from socially prescribed gender roles by voicing her truth as a girl who experienced faith so intensely that she would inspire and lead others.

The story of Rose of Viterbo is a tale of a girl's irrepressible desire to know God and her passionate expression of faith. But how we know about Rose and what we know about her goes far to explain the need for this book. While Rose was alive in the thirteenth century and in the two centuries after her death, she was known by the citizens of Viterbo as their inspiring civic preacher. Once she received official recognition as a saint in 1457, all texts, documents, and liturgies that were written to celebrate this lay Franciscan woman failed to retain references to the characteristic features of mendicancy, most notably itinerant preaching, that gives sense to her story as a lay Franciscan. Rehabilitating her story to its original fervor will bring a deeper appreciation of how laywomen participated in the Franciscan tradition at an early stage.

THE SOURCES

The life story of a young, medieval woman who died at the age of eighteen is rarely the kind of story that gets recorded. So how is it that we know about Rose? Ultimately, the answer to that question is that the people of Viterbo told and retold stories about Rose. Mothers and aunts told stories to children on their knees about the little girl who was a preacher. Lawyers and doctors talked about her and, no doubt, debated aspects of her fame while stopping to chat on street corners. And over dinner, families talked about her. The repeated act of telling stories about the girl's faith cultivated and continued the deep appreciation that the people of Viterbo had for their little saint. But still, stories like these usually remain ephemeral in the form of chatting. While most of the stories told about Rose were never written down, we do see a glimpse of them in the canonization records of the fifteenth century.[31] In these records testimonies were taken from leading citizens of the city, both men and women, all of whom talked freely and knowingly about the faith of the child even though she had died over 200 years earlier. When asked how they knew so much about her, they gave responses such as "I heard stories from my grandmother"; "My mother had told me stories when I was younger." The stories that people told about Rose fostered and sustained the girl's reputation for holiness for the two centuries between the time of her death and the time of the successful canonization. In some circles, people continue to retell these stories today.

These stories about Rose took a more complete and formal form when they were officially written down as hagiography or saint's life. One version was written immediately after her death in 1251; and another one was written over 150 years later, sometime in the early fifteenth century.[32] While hagiographies cannot be trusted to report biographical facts, they do pass on contemporary beliefs and thereby reflect the hopes and assumptions about holiness. What emerges from these sources about Rose is a picture of a medieval city's faith

---

[31] On the testimonies taken at the girl's canonization process, see G. Abate, *S. Rosa di Viterbo, Terziana Francescana: Fonti Storiche della Vita e loro Revisione critica* (Rome: Editrice Miscellanea Francescana, 1952), orig. pub. in *Miscellanea Francescana* 52, fasc. 1-2 (Jan.-Jun., 1952): 112-278 (all page references are to the monograph version), 145-60, esp. 155-60.

[32] On Rose and for the texts related to her including her hagiographies, see G. Abate, *S. Rosa di Viterbo*; Anna Maria Vacca, *La menta e la Croce* (Rome: Bulzoni, 1982); Ernesto Piacentini, *Il Libro dei miracoli di Santa Rosa di Viterbo* (Viterbo: Basilica di Francesco alla Rocca, 1991); Joan Weisenbeck and Marlene Weisenbeck, "Rose of Viterbo: Preacher and Reconciler," in *Clare of Assisi: A Medieval and Modern Woman. Clarefest Selected Papers*, ed. I. Peterson, Clare Centenary Series, vol. 8 (St. Bonaventure, NY: The Franciscan Institute, 1996), 145-55; M. d'Alatri, "Rosa di Viterbo: La santa a voce di popolo," *Italia Francescana* 44 (1969): 122-30; and Darleen Pryds, "Proclaiming Sanctity through Proscribed Acts: The Case of Rose of Viterbo," in *Women Preachers and Prophets through Two Millennia of Christianity*, 159-72. Images of Rose and her city of Viterbo, along with a translation of the thirteenth century *vita* about Rose by Joan Weisenbeck and Marlene Weisenback are available on a limited edition cd-rom, *Saint Rose of Viterbo: Preacher and Reconciler* (produced by Lisa Zmuda, 2001).

in a girl as a female mendicant – not a cloistered nun, but an itinerant preacher who just happened to be a girl.

ROSE'S STORY

The story we glean from the canonization testimonies and the hagiographies goes something like this. Ever since Rose was a young child, she was unusually sensitive with regard to things of the Spirit. As a young girl she saw visions of souls who had passed from this life to the next long before she had been born and she was able to recognize and identify them as citizens of her city. She could in fact refer to them by name, and she was able to determine who among them was good and who was bad. She performed pious acts of self-mortification and prayer at home and in public, often to the consternation of her parents, both of whom tried to moderate their daughter's devotional acts. When Rose desired to wear a hairshirt and to eat only bitter herbs, her mother urged her to stop such harsh practices. But Rose persevered and got her way. Not only was she able to wear her hairshirt, but she received the cord to cinch up her garment from a local townswoman, who apparently led the lay community of penitents.[33] When her father erupted in rage against the crowds of pious faithful who flocked to the family home to listen to Rose speak, he demanded that she stop and threatened to

---

[33] The tertiary branch, or the branch for lay people, of the Franciscan Order was emerging in the first half of the thirteenth century, and offered avenues for pious laymen and laywomen to affiliate with the order as a way to pursue a disciplined life of religious devotion. Known as penitents, these lay people might display all the trappings of a mendicant including wearing a religious habit or parts of a habit such as the cord, just as Rose appears to have done. But penitents would have lived in their family homes, and if appropriate for age and gender, they would have worked. On the penitential orders, see G. Meersemann, *Ordo Penitentialis: Confraternite e pietà dei laici nel Medioevo*. Also see André Vauchez, "Medieval Penitents," in *The Laity in the Middle Ages. Religious Beliefs and Devotional Practices*, tran. Daniel Bornstein (Notre Dame: University of Notre Dame, 1993), 119-27.

cut her hair and to tie her down. But at each threat, Rose embraced the opportunity as a chance to imitate Christ. So passionate was her faith that her father was moved to tears and eventually conceded to her wishes.

In time, the girl's ministry extended outside the home and became a public ministry of teaching and preaching. Inspired by visions she experienced of the Virgin Mary and of the crucified Christ, Rose lead her followers outside the traditional safe confines of the girl's domestic sphere into the streets of Viterbo, where she preached to all who would listen. Authorized by her visions and carrying a cross as a visual prop indicating her unique devotional abilities to all who saw her, Rose lead her pious hordes of believers through the streets, praising the name of Christ and Mary as she brought them to church. Radical in her actions of public speech and public leadership, Rose never ventured into radical theology. Instead her pious words resounded through the city as the unquestionable words inspired by none other than Christ and the Virgin Mary. Her words threatened only the imperial enemies of the Church because she posited the supremacy of divine authority against the human power of the emperor and his local minions who governed the city of Viterbo.

Having become the virtual spokesperson of the Church in her city that was ruled by imperial sympathizers, Rose was never stifled by ecclesiastical authorities. Instead, civic authorities, representing the Emperor, Frederick II, brought an end to her public exhortations in Viterbo by exiling the girl and her family, apparently because of her influence over the citizens of the city. But the family's period of exile in the surrounding countryside and nearby cities only furthered the girl's preaching career and widened her special reputation. Preaching on the authority of angels whose words she claimed to transmit, the girl spoke to enthusiastic and curious crowds. According to one account, she performed spectacular miracles such as walking through flames unscathed in an effort to demonstrate the force of her faith to convert a heretical woman. In another account Rose waxed eloquently and persuasively as she argued in theological and philosophical debates with other heretics. And most impressively, she accurately prophesied the emperor's death. When news arrived confirming her prophecy, the public's respect and awe for the girl's spiritual capacities deepened, and in a short amount of time she and her family were welcomed back to their home of Viterbo.

While one legend of her life ends here, the other tells of the girl's final years as she matured into young adulthood and of her subsequent miracles performed after her death. Fervently desiring to live out her life of religious devotion in the most traditional and respectable means possible, Rose requested permission to enter the monastery of an order of cloistered sisters connected to the network of houses founded by Clare. It was a hope that would have ended her active and public apostolate. But the young street-preacher was frustrated in her desire when the abbess told her that there was no room for her within the convent. Knowing that this was not true, Rose is said to have responded, "That which you disdain to have while living, you will rejoice to have dead, and you will have it."[34] She continued her life as a wandering preacher and prophet until she died in 1251. Within a few years, her body was exhumed, and sweet oil smelling like manna was found with her body, which was then transferred to her final resting place. Just as Rose had prophesied, the sisters of the monastery who had refused her admission while she was alive, eagerly received her incorrupt body as a holy relic, which they continue to display with both pride and protective vigilance to this day.

The relic of Rose's body has played an important role in the civic life of Viterbo since the sisters took possession of it. In addition to the annual procession of Rose's body (accompanied by a parade of floats) on the saint's feast day on September 4, the body has been used as a means of protection by the citizens of the city. In times of civic trauma and danger, such as in the wake of devastating earthquakes or military attack, citizens of Viterbo have processed the body through the city

---

[34] Abate, *S. Rosa di Viterbo,* 136.

as a prayerful means of defense and safekeeping. So even after her death, this young laywoman has served a central role in this city's life to teach, lead, and protect as she embodied mendicant spirituality.

But the fate of her reputation in official texts has strayed from her physical significance for the city and for the Franciscan tradition. While she has physically remained a central figure for Viterbo citizens, as is evidenced by her incorrupt body and by the large number of statues of her around the city even today, her reputation as written into texts has over the centuries come to minimize her Franciscan identity in its full expressions.

Immediately after her death, Rose was considered and vigorously promoted for canonization by none other than Pope Innocent IV himself. The pope had seen in Rose a strong spokesperson for the Church and an admirable counterpart to Francis to promote a female model of mendicant ideals. As a preacher, teacher, and an effective ecclesiastical spokesperson against political adversaries, Rose embodied the Franciscan charism as a laywoman in a way that was worthy of the highest spiritual honor. And yet the public way in which she expressed her faith was edgy and pushed social expectations of proper comportment for women. Rose represented a daring gamble for the choice of a female Franciscan saint. There was always the risk when canonizing a holy person that the average faithful may assume imitation rather than admiration was the appropriate response. Positioning a young female preacher as a role model could be dangerous or at least precarious. As it happened, during the course of the canonization procedure, another eminent female Franciscan who did not pose the same social threats died. Clare of Assisi, the cloistered version of feminine Franciscanism, died in 1253, and quickly provided a less controversial option to ecclesial officials. The canonization of Rose suddenly ended without a positive decision.

It would be another 200 years before Rose would be beatified through the skillful maneuvering of yet another pope, Calixtus III, in 1457. But just when Rose's official status changed, so did her reputation. Specifically, her role as a mendicant preacher was removed from official texts about the girl. The canonization bull for Rose mentions, as evidence of her holiness, ascetic acts of faith, such as fasting and self-flagellation. And, much is made of the girl's deep faith and her miraculous and profound knowledge (*miraculosae et profundae scientiae*). But nowhere is her public preaching mentioned.[35] The canonization bull codes the girl's public speech against heretics as "rebuke" and "refutation." But her inspirational preaching to the faithful is not mentioned. Rose's reputation for preaching was further suppressed in the seventeenth century because of the fate of a biography written by Isidoro Nardi. Commissioned by the abbess of the Monastery of St. Rose who sought a new work that praised the anti-heretical work of the girl, Nardi wrote a book that characterized her as nothing less than an "amazon of Christ" and labeled the city's saint an "apostolic preacher," a phrase that endangered the reputation of the book, the girl, and the entire city when it was placed on the Index of Prohibited Books until the phrase was edited out.[36] And finally, in 1952 when Pope Pius XII commemorated the 700th anniversary of the saint's death, he wrote a text that mirrored the canonization bull in highlighting the girl's asceticism and piety. Rose's public speech is referred to as "encouraging the people," "rebuking errors," and opposing tyranny. Against her tenacious adversaries, Rose "endured in silence." But Pius XII failed to mention her public leadership as preaching.[37] In short, the aspects of Rose's story concerning her active leadership, her public preaching, and her eloquent teaching and guidance have all been minimized and hidden in official, clerical statements made about her. The characteristics that made her a lay mendicant have been removed from her official story as told in texts and therefore from our understanding of the

---

[35] Abate, *S. Rosa da Viterbo*.

[36] The placement of the book on the Index was at the hands of Cardinal Urbando Sachetti in 1692; see Anna Maria Vacca, *La menta e la Croce* n.269.

[37] Abate, *S. Rosa da Viterbo*.

breadth of the mendicant movement. It is only in the stories people continue to tell about her that she is actively remembered as the mendicant laywoman she was.

CONCLUSION

Rose emerged as a most unusual religious leader in the middle of the thirteenth century, and her reputation for this leadership grew through the two centuries leading to her canonization in 1457. Situated at a time when many scholars have mapped out decreasing opportunities for women in religious leadership roles especially those in public,[38] the story of the adolescent street preacher from Viterbo requires explanation on many different levels. How is it that a young girl was able to take to the streets and preach like a friar?

In large part the audacious role taken by Rose was facilitated by her age. As a child and then as a young, unmarried woman (whose image has been consistently infantalized in art), Rose did not threaten her immediate peers like the women preachers among the Waldensians discussed above in the Introduction. As a pre-pubescent girl, Rose took a public speaking role without the kind of sexualized threat earlier Waldensian preachers leveled. About sixty years before Rose preached in the streets, Geoffrey of Auxerre had denounced women preachers as Jezebels: "Who has brought that Jezebel back to life, a young woman after a thousand years, so that she may run through the streets and squares like a prostitute preacher?"[39] But now in the middle of the thirteenth century, after Francis and his friars had established a men-

---

[38] Elizabeth Makowski depicts the thirteenth and fourteenth centuries as a period of growing repression of female activities. *Canon Law and Cloistered Women: Periculoso and its Commentators*, 1298-1545. (Washington, DC: The Catholic University of America Press, 1997), 15: "Gone were the days of the great abbesses of the early Middle Ages who routinely preached and blessed their nuns."

[39] As cited by Beverly Kienzle, "The Prostitute Preacher. Patterns of Polemic against Medieval Waldensian Women Preachers," in *Women*

dicant form of spirituality that was lived and preached in the streets, lay people, including for a time girls and women, at least those women who dared to break from social conventions and expectations like Rose, could embrace this same charism of public expression of faith. Scholars and church officials debated whether laity and especially laywomen should be able to preach. But, in pockets around Western Europe, we find women preaching. Rose is just one example.[40]

The suppression of Rose's reputation as a preacher, however, reveals the challenges facing administrators of the institutionalized church. How does a pastor or a bishop who is responsible for correct teaching regulate who can preach? The easiest approach and one that has been practiced most consistently has been to suppress preaching by laity.[41]

How a leader in any tradition is remembered depends on those who participate in that tradition. Today, among friars and lay affiliates of the Franciscans, we have choices to make about how we choose to remember Rose of Viterbo. The earliest hagiography represents her as a lay mendicant: someone who preached and inspired her contemporaries in much the same way Francis and his early followers did. Since hagiog-

---

Preachers and Prophets through Two Millennia of Christianity, 99-113, at 103.

[40] To date, the best overview in English of the situation is William Skudlarek, "Assertion without Knowledge? The Lay Preaching Controversy of the High Middle Ages," Ph.D. Dissertation, Princeton Theological Seminary, 1976. On specific women as preachers, see Roberta McKelvie, *Retrieving a Living Tradition. Angelina of Montegiove. Franciscan, Tertiary, Beguine* (St. Bonaventure, NY: Franciscan Institute, 1997); and Karen Scott, "Catherine of Siena, 'Apostola'," *Church History* 61.1 (1992): 34-46. It is clear that preaching was also performed by women outside the mendicant orders. Among them are Birgitta of Sweden and Umilta of Faenza; see Clare Sahlin, "Preaching and Prophesying: The Public Proclamation of Birgitta of Sweden's Revelations," in *Performance and Transformation, New Approaches to Late Medieval Spirituality*, ed. M. Suydam and J. Ziegler (New York: St. Martin's Press, 1999), 69-96.

[41] A brief overview of the problem through Christian history and today is mapped out by Patricia Parcahini in *Lay Preaching. State of the Question*, (Collegeville, MN: Liturgical Press, 1999). Her assessment, however, overlooks many of the windows of opportunities for lay preaching that have occurred throughout the history of the Church since her purpose in writing is to explore the present legal and theological state.

raphy is more about myth than biography, we can, at best, tell from these sources what Rose's contemporaries believed about her. They believed that she was religiously precocious and exhibited signs of unusually sensitive piety as a young child. They believed that she grew to become a charismatic public leader within her city of Viterbo by the age of about ten. And by the time of her untimely death at 18, she had already become regionally known as a persuasive expert of religious debate, a captivating street preacher, and an inspiring spiritual leader. How much of this is factual will never be known; how much of it was believed to be true is evidenced from the canonization testimonies. In short, the people of Viterbo believed Rose to be a leader who not only exhibited the holy virtues of simplicity, poverty, humility, courage, and piety, but also embodied them. By embodying them, she shared them and taught them to her contemporaries, thus becoming an influential preacher within the Franciscan intellectual tradition.

STUDY QUESTIONS

1. What active role did the friars take in Rose's early education and formation as a woman of faith?

2. When did the reputation of Rose as public preacher begin to be reduced and suppressed?

3. In what ways did Rose of Viterbo exhibit characteristics of the Franciscan life?

SPIRITUAL REFLECTION

1. The story of Rose is the story of a child's fearless ability to speak the truth against powerful leaders. Her story highlights the capacity of youth to discount established authority in order to voice their personally felt truth. Exercise: Retell

the story of a child or adolescent you know who exhibited this same kind of bold ability to speak the truth. Include in your account how adults reacted to this child's fearlessness.

2. Why do adults so often lose the fearless ability to speak their truth that Rose exhibited?

3. From what you know about Francis of Assisi and the Franciscan tradition, what are the fundamentally Franciscan characteristics about Rose's fearless ability to speak?

4. How can a fearless ability to speak be cultivated as a spiritual gift? Or is it something that is innate?

5. Adults can be afraid of the profound faith of children. Consider this statement and reflect on your experiences of the reactions of adults to children's faith.

CHAPTER THREE

ANGELA OF FOLIGNO (D. 1309)
MASTER OF THEOLOGIANS

When you're seeking advice on a problem, chances are you ask someone you think has had adequate experience to help: someone who knows firsthand the nature of the problem and can identify with your dilemma. Medieval people were no different. And when it came to religious questions and spiritual problems some people in the late thirteenth and early fourteenth century turned to Angela of Foligno in the same way twentieth century Americans turned to Abigail Van Buren in the twentieth century: they wrote letters. For this reason, Angela of Foligno could be called the "Dear Abby" of late medieval Italy.[42]

The comparison of Angela to a modern American advice columnist is especially appropriate because of the way in which women participated (and how they were allowed to participate) in the intellectual tradition of the Franciscan movement in particular, and in intellectual pursuits at all

---

[42] Abigail Van Buren, the pen name for Pauline Phillips, began a popular advice column that became syndicated in the American press in 1956. Her importance in American social history and the importance of advice columnists in general have been rigorously studied in recent years. For a discussion on the role of advice columnists in early American intellectual history, see Catherine Kerrison, *Claiming the Pen: Women and Intellectual Life in the Early American South*, (Ithaca, NY: Cornell University Press, 2006). Although medieval equivalents are rare, Angela stands out as an important example of how a woman could claim religious and social authority through letters of advice and support.

throughout much of Church history. While unable to attend classes formally at institutions of higher learning and therefore unable to study and take on the pursuits traditionally associated with theological learning, medieval women studied informally with confessors or by listening to sermons, and found outlets other than formal theological treatises in which to share their learning. Receiving letters from the faithful who sought spiritual direction and advice and responding in kind with letters is one important way in which Angela established her place in the Franciscan intellectual tradition.

A second way in which Angela participated in the intellectual tradition of the Franciscan movement was through her autobiography or spiritual memoir. This text, called the *Memorial,* reveals how Angela took in fundamental Franciscan teachings such as reflection on the Crucifixion and Passion of Christ, but then expressed this learning through the grief, suffering, and pain that she experienced through reflection. Far from being an academic text on the Passion, her rendition of it and of all Franciscan theology was expressed through a physical understanding of theology. Passionate and embodied, Angela's theological understanding was a visceral one, and she wrote about it in her *Memorial*.

Angela's exuberant expression of faith and theology can jar the unassuming reader today, which is all the more reason to remember that among her contemporaries, Angela became known as the *Magistra Theologorum*, or "Master of Theologians." Her passionate experience of spiritual beliefs and her willingness to express the challenges these experiences brought to her life made her stand out among both men and women in her day as a spiritual and intellectual master.

BIOGRAPHICAL OVERVIEW

Angela of Foligno (1248-1309) emerged as an important religious teacher and spiritual director in large part because of the complicated inner journey she herself endured. Having been married with children when she suffered a mid-life crisis that evolved into an intense religious conversion lasting several years, Angela was seen by her contemporaries as someone who had "been there," and could therefore be trusted. Her reputation was also legitimized and promoted by her close working relationship with Franciscan friars. Her voice as a spiritual director resonated uniquely among her contemporaries. As the author of her own spiritual memoir and of letters of spiritual instruction that remain extant, her voice continues to resonate uniquely today.

Angela was probably born around 1248 in Foligno, a city not far from Assisi.[43] "Lella," as she was known, was reared in a rather affluent family and married around the age of twenty. Angela was a woman from what we would call the upper-middle class. She carried out a significant number of domestic responsibilities, as a wife, mother, and caregiver for her aging mother. Then suddenly during the course of this busy life, she experienced a mid-life crisis. Her crisis turned into a profound religious conversion that fundamentally transformed her life, leading her to emotionally abandon her family much to the shock and disapproval of many of her contemporaries. From this new place in life, Angela took up a significant form of spiritual leadership that eventually led contemporaries to call her *magistra theologorum*, or "master of theologians."

How did this happen? And why do we know about Angela of Foligno? The life of an average middle class woman from medieval Umbria would usually remain unknown to us today. But Angela's close relationship with Franciscan friars facilitated her inner journey of spiritual growth that

---

[43] Brief biographical overviews of Angela can be found in the introductions of recent translations of her works: see Paul Lachance, tran., *Angela of Foligno. Complete Works* (New York: Paulist Press, 1993), 16-23; and Cristina Mazzoni, *Angela of Foligno. Memorial*, tran. John Cirignano (Cambridge: D.S. Brewer, 1999), 1-3. Paul Lachance offers a brief edition of the "highlights" of both texts in *Angela of Foligno. Passionate Mystic of the Double Abyss* (Hyde Park, New York: New City Press, 2006). All references to the translated text are taken from Lachance's full translation.

ultimately launched her into a role of religious leadership among her contemporaries which in turn tore away the average woman's veil of obscurity. The friars were responsible both for supporting and cultivating Angela's inner, spiritual world and for acting as important agents, promoting her "career" as a lay religious leader. Without the close proximity to and cooperation with the friars, Angela's life would have probably remained one of relative obscurity to history. It was the mutual influence with the friars and close cooperation with them that allowed this laywoman eventually to flourish in her faith and emerge as a lay religious leader and spiritual director. How Angela maneuvered through this period of personal transformation and stress to create a life of religious leadership is one focus of this chapter.

The other focus of this chapter examines how Angela embodied Franciscan theology especially with regard to an emphasis on the passion of Christ. Like the other Franciscan woman considered in this volume, Angela's place in the Franciscan intellectual tradition is two-fold: she embodied what she taught.

Angela lived out and taught Franciscan theology by intensely sensing and feeling the presence of Jesus and his passion in the same way Francis had done earlier in the thirteenth century. Angela's theology was a sensual one, not strictly limited to dictated words written down on parchment or limited to advice given in conversation. She experienced her theological precepts, which has brought her admirers and detractors, alike.

THE SOURCES

We know about Angela's life story and career as a spiritual director from her own autobiography, called her *Memorial*, and letters of spiritual advice she sent, which are generally referred to as her *Instructions*. These kinds of sources are unusual for the period, especially to have been written by a woman. She certainly could not have produced these on her own. And even if she had, they likely would not have remained extant. Instead, Angela had help in her writing and in the preservation of her writing. The reason either of these sources exists has to do with Angela's close working relationship with the friars at the church of San Francesco in Foligno. Angela lived near the church, which was run by the friars. Her relationship with these friars, especially with a friar who functioned as her confessor, known only as Brother A., created a support system that not only offered Angela a kind of spiritual advice, but also created a form of record keeping for her and about her once the friar realized her unusual capacity for personal spiritual growth that could in turn influence those around her. A word about each of the sources is important to understand them.[44]

Angela's *Memorial* was written sometime between 1291/1292 to 1296/1297 and is often characterized as an autobiography. One might more accurately call it an "autohagiography," since it was composed specifically to tell the story of Angela's conversion by highlighting the special, even supernatural aspects of her religious path. The fact that it was written with the help of a friar, who had an eye for promoting her as a holy woman also points to the quasi-hagiographical aspect of the work. As stated above in the introduction to this book, hagiography is an important kind of source that helps us understand what aspects and characteristics are considered holy by any culture. With Angela's *Memorial* as a lens, we see a late medieval urban society that looks increasingly to lay models of holiness.[45]

In Angela's letters known as the *Instructions*, we see the kinds of advice, teaching, and personal reflections this holy woman shared with her followers, who included laity and or-

---

[44] Both works are readily available in English translation; see Paul Lachance, tran. *Angela of Foligno. Complete Works* (New York: Paulist Press, 1993).

[45] This has been noticed by other scholars, notably André Vauchez who called the thirteenth and fourteenth centuries a heyday of lay sanctity. See *The Laity in the Middle Ages. Religious Beliefs and Devotional Practices*, 119-27.

dained. Written in the final years of her life after her conversion had been completed, once she had attained a position of recognizable spiritual authority, Angela's letters reveal descriptions of her intense physical experiences of the Divine, ranging from ecstasy to agony – sometimes both at the same time. In addition some of these letters offer concrete advice, such as her warning to priests not to let compliments of their preaching go to their heads.[46] The original letters that requested her responses do not exist, but the purpose of each note is generally clear from its internal cohesion.

Because all of Angela's writings were dictated to a friar, the role of a male amanuensis or secretary who copied down the book as dictated by Angela immediately calls into question her role as author. Most female authors of the medieval period wrote through a male secretary, since most female authors did not know how to write. Literacy of the time often included the ability to read, but failed to include the ability to write. Scholars have studied the editorial role of male secretaries and have argued that their editing in format and in language may alter the text significantly from the author's own words.[47] But, it is no different from ghostwriters today who heavily edit and present the words of famous people whose self-told stories people want to read, but whose personal talents and gifts do not include writing. So, it remains true that this is as close as we can get to female-authored voices from the period. That Angela dictated her autobiography to a friar who then edited for diction, format and organization, and perhaps, at times, for content, is something we need to remember when considering Angela as an author.

---

[46] Lachance, *Angela of Foligno*, 261-62.

[47] See esp. Catherine Mooney, "The Authorial Role of Brother A. in the Composition of Angela of Foligno's *Revelations*," in *Creative Women in Medieval and Early Modern Italy: A Religious and Artistic Renaissance*, ed. E. Ann Matter and John Coakley (Philadelphia: University of Pennsylvania Press, 1994), 34-63; and more recently John Coakley, "Hagiography and Theology in the *Memorial* of Angela of Foligno," in *Women, Men, and Spiritual Power. Female Saints and their Male Collaborators* (New York: Columbia University Press, 2006), 111-29.

The appearance and the circulation of a book written by a laywoman would have been extremely rare and would have warranted special attention. Copies of the *Memorial* are prefaced by a carefully composed list of eminent and trustworthy friars who gave special support and approval to the text of this laywoman. Shortly after its composition but before the book circulated widely, the text was read and received official approbation from Cardinal James of Colonna, an avid supporter of the Franciscans, and was endorsed by eight unnamed Franciscan theologians. While the theologians are unnamed, we know that they carried important offices which included two inquisitors, a lector at the convent in Milan, and a Provincial custodian.[48] While it is true that a book written by a laywoman would have received special scrutiny because of the rarity of such authorship, it is important not to take this official approbation as a sign of medieval or ecclesiastical misogyny. Many works authored by men have similar prefaces of approval and endorsement. Just as book covers today may have short quotes from well known and highly respected authorities to help sell a book, Angela's volume needed authoritative endorsement, as well. She was an unknown author. The list of official endorsements helped sell her book.

Even more interesting than the caveats above concerning her authorship and the endorsements is the fact that there was a market for Angela's *Memorial*. The medieval book market was not so very different from our own.[49] The market for a book drives production of a book. Books were expensive to produce. In the late thirteenth and early fourteenth centuries books were still produced on parchment or sheepskin (paper would very soon be introduced to Western Europe). Even a single copy of a book was a precious item. The fact that the life story of a laywoman would be published and cop-

---

[48] Lachance, *Angela of Foligno*, 123; this series of endorsements was left out of Mazzoni's edition.

[49] On medieval book culture, see Armando Petrucci, *Writers and Readers in Medieval Italy. Studies in the History of Written Culture* (New Haven: Yale University Press, 1995).

ies of the work would circulate is significant evidence of the special status Angela achieved during her life.

ANGELA'S STORY

We know little of Angela's life before her conversion, and what we do know about this early part of her life is often disparagingly dismissed as "sinful" from her post-conversion lens as the author of the *Memorial*. Most likely, more than living an exceedingly hedonistic life prior to her conversion, Angela lived an ordinary life as a laywoman. But the details of this life remain spare. We know that she was married, although we know little more about her husband than that he suffered her conversion with no amount of patience. We know that she had several children and that at some point her domestic responsibilities included caring for an aging mother. Like many people, she enjoyed a good meal and liked nice clothes.[50] And we know that she lived near the church of San Francesco and that the friars would obviously play a crucial role in her life after her conversion. Until her conversion, though, one may assume that the role of church in her life was nothing more than ordinary. Regular attendance at mass was common, especially for social reasons, but even more compelling for the average Christian would have been listening to friars preach in the open air piazzas. Part spectacle, part social, part inspiration, the public preaching of mendicant friars was a mainstay of thirteenth century Italian faith life.[51]

---

[50] Angela alludes to all the luxuries of life that she enjoyed prior to her conversion when she delineates all that she renounced as part of her ninth step of conversion; see Lachance, *Angela of Foligno*, 126.

[51] Eucharistic devotion was just emerging as a central aspect of Christian faith by the late thirteenth century. See R.N. Swanson, *Religion and Devotion in Europe, c. 1215-c. 1515* (Cambridge: Cambridge University Press, 1995), see esp. 137-42. On the spectacle of mendicant preaching, see Augustine Thomas, *Revival Preachers and Politics in Thirteenth Century Italy: The Great Devotion of 1233* (Oxford: Clarendon Press, 1992).

At a certain point in mid-life, probably around 1292, perhaps when she was around forty years old, Angela experienced a profound conversion which she maps out as a series of stages in her *Memorial*.[52] While no attempt will be made here to repeat the entire series of stages to her conversion, it is important to highlight a few key episodes.

Her conversion seems to have begun with an inner turmoil over what she perceived as her sinful nature which led to her deep fear of damnation.[53] She immediately sought out a confessor among the friars at San Francesco who could accompany her on her spiritual path. Her own conversion took a fair amount of time – twenty-seven steps in all or about four years – and took a toll on Angela. Emotional outbursts and episodic weeping were common results of her constant bouts of self-loathing and self-condemnation.

The emotional aspects of Angela's conversion were compounded or instigated by her devotional practices focused on the passion of Christ. One practice was her habit of gazing on a crucifix she had in a room. It was this gazing on the image of the suffering Christ that allowed Angela to internalize Christ's suffering as her own. She grew to empathize so completely with him that she yearned to make a physical vow of renunciation to show her devotion:

> In the eighth step, while looking at the cross, I was given an even greater perception of the way the Son of God had died for our sins. This perception made me aware of all my sins, and this was extremely painful. I felt that I myself had crucified Christ. But I still did not know which was the greatest gift he had bestowed – whether it was the fact that he had withdrawn me from sin and hell and converted me

---

[52] The presentation of her conversion as a series of stages appears to be an imposition of structure probably given to her life story by her male secretary who heard her dictation. The structure seems strikingly scholastic, and it remains improbable that Angela herself, as a laywoman, would have conceived of her faith journey in this way.

[53] Paul Lachance, *Angela of Foligno*, 124.

to the way of penance or that he had been crucified for me. Nonetheless, this perception of the meaning of the cross set me so afire that, standing near the cross, I stripped myself of all my clothing and offered my whole self to him. Although very fearful, I promised him then to maintain perpetual chastity and not to offend him again with any of my bodily members, accusing each of these one by one.... On the one hand I feared to make this promise, but on the other hand, the fire of which I spoke drew it out of me, and I could not do otherwise.[54]

In making this grand gesture of renunciation by stripping naked, Angela may have consciously modeled herself on Francis directly. The famous iconic scene of Francis stripping himself of his clothes in front of the bishop as a grand gesture of renouncing his parents' wealth, their way of life, and all personal claims to inherit such a life had already become well known by the late thirteenth century.[55] Scholars have noted the similarity between Francis's and Angela's respective gestures.[56]

But Angela went even further in her renunciation with a prayer that shocks readers today. Angela's complete personal renunciation comes in the context of her ninth step of conversion as she sought the way of the cross. In addition to stripping herself of all the possessions – her nice clothes and fine foods – she discerned a need to strip herself of all personal attachments, including all her personal relationships, so that, as she writes, "I would be free to give my heart to Christ from whom I had received so many graces, and to walk along the thorny path, that is the path of tribulation."[57] And then, her life suddenly changed:

---

[54] Paul Lachance, *Angela of Foligno*, 125-26. Angela used gazing on the cross or on a crucifix as a form of meditation frequently; cf. 175-76.

[55] The scene had already become standard in the early hagiographies of Francis; 1C15; 2C12; LMaj 2; L3C 6: 20.

[56] Paul Lachance, *Angela of Foligno*, 366-67, n. 9.

[57] Paul Lachance, *Angela of Foligno*, 126.

[I]t came to pass, God so willing, that at that time my mother, who had been a great obstacle to me, died. In like manner my husband died, as did all my sons in a short space of time. Because I had already entered the aforesaid way, and had prayed to God for their death, I felt a great consolation when it happened. I thought that since God had conceded me this aforesaid favor, my heart would always be within God's heart, and God's heart always within mine.[58]

The passage can take your breath away with its brutal honesty. The truth this passage reveals points to the inner tensions and very real anguish religious conversion can cause. In the case of Angela, living as she did in late medieval Italy, her comments here point to the tensions she felt while enduring this conversion and still finding herself with multiple domestic responsibilities which she perceived as inhibiting her spiritual progress. At that time the spiritual life was still perceived as a prerogative of men and women who were vowed religious, usually living within monastic walls. Even with the plethora of lay spiritual communities that had been fostered through the apostolic movements since the twelfth century, the vast majority of these communities continued to assume members living a single life.[59] It is little wonder that Angela felt stymied in her religious path given her domestic situation. Of equal importance is to bring attention to the fact that Angela's amanuensis/editor did not consider that the brutal truth of Angela's prayer warranted expurgation from the text, despite his probable motives of ultimately claiming official sanctity for her. Brother A. had no intention of sugar coating Angela's story. He allowed the account of her conversion to remain as raw and edgy as she experienced it.

---

[58] Lachance, *Angela of Foligno*, 126. While this passage reads in a very matter-of-fact tone, it is clear that Angela suffered deeply from her loss. Cf. Paul Lachance, *Angela of Foligno*, 143.

[59] A notable exception to this is found among the Humiliati in Lombardy. This group included married couples with families. See Herbert Grundmann, *Religious Movements in the Middle Ages*, tran. Steven Rowan (Notre Dame: University of Notre Dame, 1995), 28-40.

In many of the remaining steps Angela's conversion, the focus of her contemplation is the crucified Christ. In step ten, as a response to her prayers concerning what she could do for God, he appeared to her crucified on the cross while she was awake and while she was asleep.[60] As he showed her his many wounds, she became aware that through her sins, she had inflicted the wounds anew on Christ. Realizing that there was nothing she could do to satisfy her own guilt for such pain and suffering, she responded with physical emotional outbursts: "I wept much, shedding hot tears that burned my flesh. I had to apply water to cool it."[61] And in even a more graphic response, Angela later in the fourteenth step saw the crucified Christ as she stood in prayer. "He then called me to place my mouth to the wound in his side. It seemed to me that I saw and drank the blood, which was freshly flowing from his side."[62]

These graphic images in Angela's faith journey were not gratuitous. Instead they brought about the cultivation of Angela's deeply felt compassion for those who suffer and her deep sense of humility which she tried to instill in her followers. On the one hand these sensual experiences with Christ crucified gave her the opportunities to feel empathy with his suffering. In turn she rededicated her life to serving others through charitable service at a local hospital where she helped raise funds to feed patients and bathe lepers[63] and through her own spiritual direction to her followers. Her meditations on Christ's suffering first and foremost cultivat-

---

[60] Paul Lachance, *Angela of Foligno*, 126-27.

[61] Paul Lachance, *Angela of Foligno*, 127.

[62] Paul Lachance, *Angela of Foligno*, 128. A similar image is found in Angela's *Instructions* where she recounts her experience of the crucified Christ during the celebration of Mass. In her detailed description of the wounded and bloody Christ, Angela recounts her seeing Christ reach down and bring the heads of her followers to kiss his wound. See Paul Lachance, *Angela of Foligno*, 245-46. While perhaps shocking to the modern reader, this image of drinking Christ's blood directly from his side is found in texts related to other medieval mystics around the same time, including Margaret of Cortona and Catherine of Siena. Paul Lachance, *Angela of Foligno*, 368, n. 15.

[63] Paul Lachance, *Angela of Foligno*, 162-63.

ed in Angela a sense of personal humility, so that her service and teaching were done without arrogance or pride, a theme she stressed with her followers, especially those who were ordained:

> Behold, my blessed sons, and observe the model of your life, the suffering God and man, and learn from him the form of all perfection. Observe his life, be attentive to his teachings, and with all your affection, run after him, so that led by him you may successfully attain the cross. He gave himself as an example and exhorts us to look at him with the eye of the spirit as he says, 'Learn from me for I am meek and humble of heart and you will find rest for your souls.'

> My sons, be attentive, look with your most profound gaze into the depths of this doctrine, the sublimity of this teaching. Note its bases and its roots. Christ did not say: 'Learn from me to fast,' although as an example to us and for our salvation, he fasted forty days and forty nights.... He did not say: 'Learn from me to despise the world and to live in poverty,' although he lived in very great poverty and wished that his disciples live in the same way.... But he said simply 'Learn from me because I am meek and humble of heart.' The truth of the matter is that he set forth humility of heart and meekness as the foundation and firmest basis for all the other virtues ...[64]

Thus, from a position of humility grounded in her devotional practice of meditating on the passion of Christ, Angela established herself as an adviser, teacher, and helper among her peers who included laymen, laywomen, friars, and ordained men.

---

[64] Paul Lachance, *Angela of Foligno*, 251-52. At times her advice to ordained men could be even more direct as when she told them not to let their heads be turned around by flattering comments after one preaches (Lachance, 261-62).

CONCLUSION

The extent and range of Angela's spiritual texts provide a rare glimpse into the teaching habits of this lay Franciscan woman, and thus into the role of a laywoman in the Franciscan intellectual tradition. Not shy about sharing her visceral experiences of prayer and meditation, Angela reveled in the details of her encounters especially with the crucified Christ. With the shrewd assistance of her confessor, these experiences bolstered Angela's personal authority as a woman of special spiritual capacity and, as a result, a woman with teachings that warranted careful attention. Never having studied formally at a university or school of the order, Angela, nevertheless, earned a reputation as someone with credentials of learning that came from her innate intelligence, diligent informal study, and confident appropriation of ideas. Without a doubt, her reputation was cultivated through her special relationship with the friars, especially with the close working relationship she shared with Brother A. who patiently worked with his passionate charge. Without the friars, Angela would have slipped into oblivion like that vast majority of women in history. With the friars, she earned the role as an influential teacher and adviser to her contemporaries. As this influential teacher, Angela thus earns an important place in the intellectual tradition of the order.

STUDY QUESTIONS

1. What factors made Angela's spiritual authority recognized and accepted by her contemporaries?

2. How did Angela's affiliation with the friars affect her "career"?

REFLECTION QUESTIONS

1. If you were to write a letter of spiritual advice to your parish priest or local minister, what would it say?

2. Practice Angela's form of prayer and mediation by gazing on a crucifix for a period of time, such as fifteen-thirty minutes. How does gazing affect you as a form of prayer?

3. Angela could be brutally honest in revealing her inner struggle that emerged with her religious conversion. Reflect on your own willingness to be so honest about your struggles. And consider whether you are willing to listen without casting judgment as others honestly reveal their own struggles in faith. Describe the courage it takes to be so honest.

CHAPTER FOUR

MARGARET OF CORTONA (D. 1297)
THE *POVERELLA*

Today most people outside of the Tuscan city of Cortona
have rarely heard of that city's medieval patron saint, Margaret. But in the late thirteenth century, Margaret of Cortona was so famous she was considered the founder of the
third branch of the Franciscan family, the lay associates. So,
next to Francis, who was the founder of the friars, which was
considered to be the "first order" of Franciscans, and next to
Clare, the founder of the "second order" of nuns, was Margaret in a triumvirate of leadership in the Franciscan family.
As a lay Franciscan, Margaret came to symbolize the Franciscan charism so closely that her biographer called her "Poverella," spinning a feminine form of Francis's own nickname,
the "Poverello."[65] Yet despite her historical prominence and

---

[65] All references to the life of Margaret of Cortona written by Giunta
Bevegnati are taken from the edition found in *Antica leggenda della vita
e dei miracoli di Santa Marherita da Cortona* (Lucca, 1793; rpt. Siena,
1897), see 1:1, 2 for the reference to Margaret as the "Poverella" of Christ.
More recently, see Fortunato Iozzelli, ed., *Iunctae Bevegnatis. Legenda de
Vita et Miraculis Beatae Margaritae de Cortona*, Bibliotheca franciscana
ascetica medii aevi 13 (Grottaferrata: Editiones Collegii S. Bonaventurae
ad Claras Aquas, 1997). For a brief summary of her life, see B. Schlager,
"Foundress of the Franciscan Life: Umiliani Cerchi and Margaret of Cortona," *Viator* 29 (1998): 141-66 at 157-66. Also see John Coakley, "The Lim-
its of Religious Authority: Margaret of Cortona and Giunta Bevegnati," in
*Women, Men and Spiritual Power. Female Saints and their Male Counter-
parts,* 130-48.

influence within the Franciscan tradition, her story remains
little known outside of academic circles.

This chapter offers an introduction to her life to help re-
broadcast the story of this lay Franciscan leader. In addition
this chapter will examine a particular theme that her relationship within the Franciscan family projects. Margaret's relationship with the Franciscan Order was not always smooth
or close. Margaret's story reveals the realities of religious
and laity working, praying, and living in close relationship:
at times the relationship strains and at other times the relationship breaks. But one of the things that is reflected most
clearly in Margaret's life is her on-going efforts to search for
a way to find religious truth alone and in community. How
Margaret sought to live a lay life in cooperation and in mutual respect with vowed religious is a primary lesson that
can be extracted from Margaret's life as a lay Franciscan.

SOURCES

First a word about how we know Margaret's story is in
order. Just like Rose of Viterbo, Margaret emerged as a local religious celebrity and was generally admired as a holy
woman. Shortly after her death at the age of fifty in 1297, a
Franciscan friar, Giunta Bevegnati, wrote her life story. As
a piece a hagiography, the work is intended to cultivate the
widespread belief of Margaret as someone worthy of official
recognition as a saint. The work never circulated very widely
outside of Cortona and its immediate environs, but it remains
significant that a friar wrote a hagiographic work about one
of the lay affiliates of his order.[66] It is even more significant
that the work was approved by the most important civil and
religious officials of the day in a ceremony held at the palazzo

---

[66] Only three manuscripts of the work remain extant, which leads
scholars to deduce the work did not circulate widely. See Cannon and Vauchez, 22.

of a Cortona Lord, Uguccio Casalli, on February 15, 1308.[67] Margaret held, for the friars and for the city of Cortona, a significance that wielded influence, spiritual prestige, and potentially power.

Giunta, no doubt, had added incentive for promoting Margaret as a holy woman since he had been her spiritual director. Aside from any potential boost to Giunta's own career as a confessor and spiritual director, the canonization of Margaret would have highlighted the Franciscan Order since the friars had been so influential in Margaret's development as a religious leader. Noting these historical factors that surround the writing of Margaret's life story should not take away from her reputation as a significant religious leader of her day. They do, however, provide an important lens through which we can read her story: Margaret was depicted as a mendicant woman by a mendicant friar. Her story was one that a friar considered important to tell, since it illustrated how the friars' call and mission could be lived out beyond the order of men by a laywoman. At least in the late thirteenth century, there was an enthusiasm about the possibility of a religious ideal that could both men and women, vowed and lay, could embrace.

MARGARET'S STORY

Margaret was born around 1247 in Laviano, a small town in Umbria. As a young woman she became the mistress of a nobleman from Montepulciano. They lived together for nine years and had a son together. They never officially married, perhaps due to disparity in social and economic class which made the legal bond of marriage implausible or impractical. But clearly they lived together as common-law husband and wife without public scandal. Crisis erupted for Margaret, however, when her companion suddenly died. Brutally

---

[67] Cannon and Vauchez, 15.

attacked by robbers, he was left to die in a ditch. Margaret's discovery of his decayed body shocked her into a spiritual journey that she could not have anticipated. But the personal trauma of finding her lover's corpse was then compounded by the social and economic realities of never having married. Suddenly she was left by life's circumstances alone, impoverished, and completely disenfranchised. Stripped of all its social and economic comforts, Margaret's life suddenly embodied the core tenet of Franciscan theology: poverty.

While Francis himself had voluntarily renounced the wealth and social support of his middle class life, Margaret was thrust into this precarious position involuntarily. Without having the legal and sacramental bond of marriage, Margaret found herself without rights to inherit, so she was left without any financial support. When she tried to return to her family of birth, they refused to take her back, so she was left without a home and without a family or any form of personal or social support system. Completely disenfranchised, she moved with her young son to Cortona in Tuscany. Why she chose Cortona is unclear, but there she encountered the help of devout noblewomen who helped Margaret and her son. The kindness of these strangers helped Margaret regroup and start a new life. But what exactly did these women do to help Margaret?

Although the extant biography of Margaret is silent on these kinds of details, one can assume that these noblewomen housed Margaret, fed her, and clothed her. While providing for Margaret's material needs, these women likely listened to her as she told them about her situation as a single mother suddenly alone. And they probably consoled Margaret as she included in her stories the life-changing shock of finding her companion's rotting body. And very likely, they held her hand and sat with her in silence and in prayer. These details are all conjecture, of course. Margaret's biographer failed to include details about the nature of these days and weeks during which these nameless women gave aid and support to Margaret. His silence on their extraordinary acts of charity warrants special attention here because of the nature of this book. The large and small acts of kindness given by women throughout history have usually gone unrecorded or under-appreciated in historical sources. But in this case, two un-named noble women did nothing less than save a woman's life by taking a stranger and her young son in and caring for them. And, it is likely they saw in her the potential of becoming a woman of faith, for as the story goes, Margaret developed a strong devotional life and in time requested to wear the habit of the lay Franciscans, also known as the "penitents."

It is at this point in Margaret's life story that we see the first evidence of tension with the friars. Far from eager to ac-cept this new stranger into their group of lay affiliates, the friars remained skeptical of the woman's conversion and were suspicious that she might return to a life of sin and cause scandal in their midst as a seductress. Her plea to them to allow her to wear the penitent's habit is poignant. Giunta, in an effort to entice the empathy of his readers, describes the scenario as follows:

> How can it be that the friars delayed in granting her the habit? It is because they doubted her perseverance because she was too beautiful or too young. Afterwards, they saw that she had given herself up to Christ inseparably, and they saw that she continued to come closer to God with a sincere Spirit. One day, they heard her say: 'My fathers, the Lord entrusted me to you. Don't distrust me, since I would still love God the Almighty even if I were to spend all my life in a great desert. After you have seen me flee from the world and live among religious people and transform my life for the better through Christ's grace, why are you afraid? Why do you postpone my investiture?' At that moment, the friars, through the love of him who had vested her in his grace, granted her the habit.[68]

---

[68] *Vita*, 1:3.7.

It is noteworthy that Giunta admits that the friars doubted Margaret's call because of her beauty and her age. No doubt reservations really point to concerns about themselves, fearing the temptation of a young and beautiful woman among their lay affiliates. It has already been noted that this kind of self-distrust among the friars that was in turn outwardly directed toward women circulated among the friars in the thirteenth century.[69] Margaret's experience of the friars' distrust offers a concrete example that illustrates the challenge women faced in fulfilling their vocations as mendicants. While it is common for readers today to respond to accounts of this kind of challenge with anger and frustration, it is more fruitful to highlight Margaret's conviction, humility, and perseverance when faced with suspicion and obstacles to her religious yearnings. For in time, Margaret was admitted to the penitents and led her life in prayer and service.

After Margaret's admission to the lay penitents, she led a life that combined active ministry and solitary contemplation.[70] Her active ministry revolved around healthcare. First she worked as a midwife to noblewomen giving birth, and then she turned to helping the poor who were ill. Through her connections with noblewomen in Cortona, she founded a hospital dedicated to caring for the poor who were ill. Much of the day to day work that Margaret did herself and that she facilitated through the hospital is left to our imagination. But it does not take much imagination to appreciate her dedication to helping others, especially the poor, in their times of need.

In this capacity, we do see glimpses of how Margaret saw the need to blend spiritual care with medical care, since she apparently had made a habit of baptizing infants she helped deliver. We learn of this activity when her biographer notes

---

[69] See Introduction, n. 17.

[70] Margaret's son had been sent to be reared in a monastery, as was rather common at the time among both men and women who endured religious conversions. While active charity work was condoned among lay religious, the tasks of parenthood were obviously considered inimical to the religious life – even lay religious life.

that she gave it up since it occupied too much of her time. This remark reveals just how popular she had become as a spiritual and medical help to poor women in Cortona. The role of lay people administering baptism had been rather common, but by the later middle ages, the ordinary procedure for baptism was through a priest. Church law always allowed for the extraordinary role of the laity in this sacramental function to secure salvation for the souls of infants.[71] Margaret's role in this was more than "extraordinary." Women apparently sought her out to baptize their infants. While Margaret's biographer claims she gave up baptizing infants because it took up too much of her time, it is more likely that the friars themselves were increasingly uncomfortable with one of their lay affiliates – especially a female affiliate – taking on a sacramental task that was increasingly reserved for the ordained. We see here in Margaret's life the tensions that surfaced from the emergence of lay spiritual leaders and the rise of priest-centered faith. While people flocked to receive spiritual advice and official works of faith from lay leaders, official clerical efforts were made to curtail lay leadership. Official action against Margaret was not taken, it seems. Instead, out of a desire for obedience to the friars, she stopped baptizing infants. As is often the case in situations like this, though, she was still sought out long after she ended her ministry. In one story told by Giunta, the mother of a friar came to her for the baptism of a grandson. After performing the baptism, Margaret was apparently overcome with guilt and spent a sleepless night in her cell until she was consoled by a vision of Christ who urged her to end the baptisms.

Margaret's baptizing activity was not public per se but it certainly was not private. Word of mouth had broadcast her private liturgical actions precisely because these actions met the pastoral needs of the faithful in her community. There was a spiritual yearning among parents, especially mothers of infants, that Margaret was able to meet. While the details of how she performed these baptisms are undocumented, we

---

[71] R.N. Swanson, *Religion and Devotion in Europe, c. 1215-1515*, see esp. 31.

can presume that she reached out in concrete ways that met the spiritual needs of parents of newborns.

Much more public, however, was Margaret's tendency to perform public gestures of penance. Much like Rose's public preaching, Margaret took to the streets of Cortona to express deep felt remorse for her sins and to encourage others to penance. In the streets of Cortona, where she already arrived completely disenfranchised, she announced publicly that she deserved expulsion form the city because of the depravity of her sins. In her former city of Montepulciano, she demonstrated her deeply felt humility even more dramatically: having shaved her head she processed through the streets with a noose hung around her neck. Such public displays of penance would be readily interpreted today as unhealthy self-hatred, and she would likely be medicated for a psychological imbalance. Among her contemporaries, Margaret's behavior received a wide range of responses: some people ridiculed her, while others watched in awe of her humility and courage. Her confessor urged her to end the public displays, since he believed them to be unhealthy and made her the object of mockery. She ultimately did end these dramatic public displays, but just like Francis's public stripping of his clothes, Margaret's public processions stuck in the imagination of local faithful as the dramatic display of faith and humility performed by a charismatic lay woman.

Margaret's work in the city of Cortona was not limited to public displays of faith. Much like Angela of Foligno, about whom we read above, Margaret acted as a spiritual advisor, whose fame stretched far beyond Cortona. According to Giunta, people throughout Italy and from as far away as Spain contacted Margaret for advice on spiritual matters. Her reputation for wise spiritual counsel as well as sound practical advice started in Cortona itself where she was accepted as a mediator between factions, including those between the bishop and the citizens of the city.

Her special capacity for advice-giving, however, was within the context of healing works. Giunta specifically mentions how she could reach out and effectively communicate with women of all classes. First through her active ministry of health care, and then in those moments of helping, Margaret touched the hearts and souls of women she cared for with her faith, and brought about spiritual transformations. In addition, she worked with the friars, nursing them during sickness and listening to them as a spiritual director. Her pastoral instincts were consistent: she offered what others needed.

A great deal is made of her Franciscan devotion in the biography written by Giunta. He describes her as a woman who fervently prays to "Holy Father Francis." And the very nature of her piety shares characteristics of Franciscan devotions, especially with regard to poverty including social disenfranchisement, especially from one's family and with regard to the passion of Christ. Because of this and because of her affiliations with the friars through the lay penitentials, her departure from the Franciscan fold near the end of her life is puzzling. Near the end of her life, there is a sudden and dramatic shift in the spiritual direction of Margaret's spiritual life. Since she had arrived in Cortona, the focus of her life had been first with the Franciscan laity and ultimately with the friars themselves. But a year before she died, she moved her private cell away from the Franciscan church within Cortona to that of a diocesan church, San Basilio, just outside the city proper but still within the walled confines of Cortona.[72] High up on a hill, the church was visible to the rest of the city. Once Margaret withdrew to the cell in that church, she became a highly visible recluse. Her break with the Franciscans was publicly announced by her new residence. More privately, this break was confirmed when she turned to the spiritual advice of a new confessor who was a secular priest and not a Franciscan.

We are limited by the sources available to us to explain this shift in her life, and since the sources, most notably the biography, are penned by a Franciscan, many of the questions we may have will never be answered beyond conjec-

---

[72] For a map of medieval Cortona which highlights the position of the main churches related to Margaret's life, see Cannon and Vauchez, 10.

ture. Did Margaret have a falling out with the friars? Was she tired of following the regulations they had placed on her? Did she feel called to pick up some of her ministries, such as baptizing infants that she had to abandon under Franciscan direction? Or was she tired of the attention and fame that came from living in the middle of the city, and chose instead a quieter church outside city boundaries where she could delve into contemplative solitude without the demands of ministry? Did she choose to remove herself from close proximity to the friars in order to reduce their internal conflicts over affiliating with her? While it is possible to speculate about these questions, it remains impossible to answer any of them with precision.

On the one hand we know that Margaret took an active role in the lives of some of the friars. Her biographer relates stories of her nursing friars when they were ill and acting as their spiritual directors in times of doubt or troubles. One friar doubted that he should take communion daily, worrying he was not worthy of the daily sacrament. Margaret counseled him and assured him that God wanted him to partake in the sacrament as often as he desired to.[73] Another friar doubted his worthiness to celebrate daily Mass, which Margaret countered with general encouragement of his worthiness and firm direction to him to confess his sins before each Mass.[74] More generally and perhaps ironically, she gave advice to the friars on how to handle candidates to the lay penitents: take the acceptable candidates and refuse the weaker ones, regardless of who they are.[75] And perhaps touching on sensitive nerves, she advised the friars on the qualities that make a good friar, and she instructed the friars on how to preach. She especially urged them to preach from Scripture, specifically from the Gospels and the Pauline Letters, and she warned them to avoid becoming too chatty in their sermons.[76]

---

[73] *Vita*, 9:2, 229-30.
[74] *Vita*, 9:6, 233.
[75] *Vita*, 5:14, 93.
[76] *Vita*, 7: 23, 185.

No one likes a busybody. And it may very well be that Margaret's persistent advice-giving and on-going presence among the friars bred resentment in their midst. What we do know is that some of the friars did not appreciate Margaret's close rapport with the order. Some of them actually questioned the sincerity of her piety and doubted the veracity of her claims to have received visions. Some friars thought that her reputation for holiness was trumped up and fraudulent, and so they feared she could damage the reputation of the order should her fraud become the subject of gossip. The seriousness of this issue is evidenced by the fact that the friars discussed the subject of the order's rapport with Margaret at a chapter meeting, where it was decided that her Franciscan confessor, Giunta, should limit his visits with her to once a week.[77]

But while there was tension over her affiliation with the order during her life, it is clear that even before she died, but after Margaret left the Franciscan fold, some of the Franciscans desperately wanted to claim Margaret as one of their own. Their efforts to do so only intensified after her death when speculation circulated about her candidacy for sainthood. Her fame as a holy woman had become intense locally and had traveled some distance. To claim her as a Franciscan lay saint would help further the Franciscan message and would certainly bring praise to the order. The friars had clearly developed a close relationship with her, so that the reasons for promoting her case for sanctity and the reasons for claiming her as a lay Franciscan are not cynically political.

Nevertheless, it is important to point out these political rough edges to Margaret's fate as a lay Franciscan, since the cooperative life of laity and vowed religious does not always flow smoothly. As in any human relationship there can be tensions and even separations. The spiritual bonds that link laity and religious communities endure the same challenges. Acknowledging them as a historical reality in the case of

---

[77] *Vita*, 5:9, 82.

Margaret and the friars may be sufficient to help appreciate that conflict and its resolution are a natural part of the lay affiliation with vowed religious and can actually facilitate the process of on-going discernment for spiritual growth for all concerned.

In conclusion, Margaret's life was one of abandonment, redemption, and, ultimately, leadership. Disenfranchised and left alone as a single mother, Margaret, over time, crafted for herself with the help of pious women around her a life infused with aspects of the Franciscan charism, namely poverty, charity, and solitary contemplation. Grounded in this charism, Margaret's spiritual life propelled her into public religious leadership as a lay minister within her community. Despite conflicts with the friars, Margaret's pastoral leadership made her known by contemporaries as nothing less than the founder of the lay branch of Franciscans. Such is the life of a Franciscan laywoman: out of absolute poverty Margaret grew into a leader of prominence.

STUDY QUESTIONS

1. What factors may have caused the tensions between Margaret and the friars?

2. Consider what may have inspired Giunta to write down the story of Margaret? How did he and the friars benefit from Margaret's story being preserved?

3. After she became a hermit, Margaret remained famous in Cortona, since her hermitage was visible from the town. What is the nature of the public life of a hermit? What was her public role and influence?

REFLECTION QUESTIONS

1. Have you ever encountered someone of deep faith like the two anonymous women who took care of Margaret when she arrived in Cortona? If so, tell their story and include examples of what they did that demonstrated their faith.

2. Why do you think anonymous or hidden people like hermits can play a strong role in our faith life?

3. Is conflict between laity and clergy common? Is it inevitable? Why or why not?

4. Write a hagiography of someone you believe to be holy. You can do this either alone or with a group of people. If you are with a group, compare hagiographies and discuss the differences. What do these differences and similarities say about your views of holiness?

CHAPTER FIVE

SANCIA, QUEEN OF NAPLES (D. 1345)
PROTECTOR OF THE ORDERS

... [A] mother loves her sons, and so I love my sons, the
Friars Minor ... Sancia, by the grace of God queen of
Jerusalem and Sicily [Naples], your humble servant
and devoted daughter sends greetings in the Lord Jesus Christ ...[78]

When Sancia, queen of Naples, addressed the General
Chapter of the Franciscan Order that was meeting in Paris
in 1329, she used these warm and maternal words to greet
them. The particular words she chose to address the friars
allowed her to position herself as someone uniquely devoted
to the way of St. Francis, and thereby to the order, itself. As
queen of the Kingdom of Naples (referred to by contemporaries as the Kingdom of Sicily), Sancia held a privileged office of power, prestige, and influence, which she used to participate in the affairs of religious orders that she particularly
favored, especially the Franciscans. Sancia wielded her power
to affect official decisions of the order, and more importantly,
to affect how Franciscan ideals and policies were actually
followed by members of the order residing in her realm. She
had established a court that was friendly and supportive to

---

[78] As translated by Ronald G. Musto, "Queen Sancia of Naples (1286-
1345) and the Spiritual Franciscans," in *Women of the Medieval World. Essays in Honor of John H. Mundy*, ed. Julius Kirshner and Suzanne Wemple
(Oxford: Blackwell, 1985), 179-214, at 210.

a wide range of Franciscan causes. With personal conviction and in the apparent absence of fear, Sancia used her office as queen to establish, protect, and nurture a particular course of Franciscan piety. Her personal piety became the cornerstone of her political agenda – an agenda that she often shared with her husband, Robert, the King of Naples.

Our fourth Franciscan woman to be discussed in this volume differs from the other three by her rank and class, but shares with them the fervor of a religious faith based on a passion for Franciscan spirituality. Sancia dedicated her particular Franciscan piety to poverty and then turned this piety into a royal agenda for patronage programs and, eventually, for protocol for court life. Thus, she used her station in life to advance and extend the sphere of influence of her personal spirituality.

Today Sancia might be glibly labeled as a "poor little rich girl." Known as Sancia of Majorca or Sancia of Naples, she was born into the royal family of the Mediterranean kingdom of Majorca. In keeping with her lineage, she was expected to marry at her rank, to produce royal heirs, and to oversee a royal court. In such a life, Sancia would live surrounded by the opulence of court life with all of its extravagant food and fine dresses; its social culture and strict protocol of behavior and personal interaction; and a number of servants to do one's every bidding.

But by all accounts Sancia yearned for a different kind of life – one that centered on a simple life of prayer, away from the luxuries of court life and fawning courtiers. On several occasions she tried to quit her royal life in favor of a vowed religious life, even wearing the habit of a vowed Poor Clare sister. But it wasn't until the very end of her life that her efforts proved successful. Instead of the austere life as a vowed nun, she remained a queen at the center of one of the most culturally vibrant courts of Europe at the time. While she may have yearned for the daily sequences of prayer that characterizes cloistered life, she experienced the regular sequences of royal rituals made up of diplomatic visits, royal pageantry, and the multitude of preparations for warfare and galas.

Both forms of life – the religious and royal – center on ritual. Her personal preference was toward pious ritual rather than political and social rituals. When she was not allowed to adopt a strict life of pious ritual, she manipulated her political life to serve her religious yearnings. She did as many laywomen learn to do even today: she accommodated the particular life she found herself in to fit her innermost call and adapted her innermost call to fit within the royal life she was born into. In short, she crafted a life that she could claim was authentically her own, despite the limitations of some forms of personal freedom imposed by the circumstances in which she found herself.

SOURCES

The sources we have to learn about Sancia's life are different from those for the other three women in this volume. Unlike the earlier Franciscan women studied here, Sancia was never officially recognized as a saint. Although family members initiated an effort to seek her canonization shortly after the queen died, the cause ended quickly without sufficient evidence having been brought forward. The result for those of us trying to learn about Sancia's life is that we have very different sources to work from than we had for Rose, Angela, and Margaret. There is no hagiography of Sancia. Similarly, Sancia was never the focus of an official biography, either. Instead, the details of Sancia's life can be pasted together from traditional royal sources, namely chronicles of her family and the Angevin family into which she married; official letters she wrote or which she received that warranted preservation; and official documents, such as foundation charters of religious houses she established or supported.[79]

---

[79] For a brief overview of the extant sources concerning Sancia, see Musto, "Queen Sancia of Naples (1286-1345)."

Just like the hagiographic sources used to profile our other lay Franciscan women, the sources for Sancia reveal a particular picture of the woman and need to be used with some analytical care. The letters we have are not personal letters, but, instead, are official letters. They include letters from Sancia to the Franciscan Order, in which she makes the equivalent of "policy statements" – that is official statements that delineate her relationship to the Order. In addition there are letters back and forth to Pope John XXII which convey their argument over her desire to become a Poor Clare nun. None of these letters reveal her innermost personal thoughts or feelings about the direction her life had taken. But, analogous to the use of hagiography in the preceding chapters to find hints of the tradition of Franciscan lay women, these letters and chronicles can be used to see how this particular lay Franciscan crafted a life of devotion in spite of and with the help of her office as queen.

SANCIA'S LIFE STORY

Sancia's spiritual longings may have been innate, but they were also clearly cultivated in her family which had a reputation as being a family with strong spiritual impulses. First and foremost, Sancia's mother, Sclaramonda of Foix, was by all accounts an exceptionally pious woman who established a firm spiritual foundation to her children's upbringing. In a letter dated 1316 and addressed to the Franciscan Order, Sancia attributed her own religious devotion with its particular Franciscan bent to her mother. But the letter, which reads like a document delineating the queen's spiritual pedigree, also highlighted the number of her relatives and ancestors who were similarly driven by Franciscan piety:

Know, fathers, that for this God caused me to be born into this world from such a lineage and family tree, just as was Lady Sclaramonda of holy memory, my lady mother, queen of Majorca and true daughter of blessed Francis. He also caused that my firstborn brother, namely Friar James of Majorca, my dearest brother, renounced royal power for the love of Jesus Christ and become a son of blessed Francis and entered his order. He also caused me to be a descendent of blessed Elizabeth [of Hungary], who was such a true and devoted daughter of blessed Francis and a mother of his order. She was the blood sister of the lady mother of my father, Lord James, well-remembered King of Majorca.[80]

There is a tone of name dropping in Sancia's letter that reveals her efforts to establish her credibility with the friars through ancestral ties. She exudes familial pride when she points to her immediate family with her mother and eldest brother as prominent figures within the Franciscan family, and to her great-aunt, Elizabeth of Hungary, who by this time was already a canonized follower of Francis. She could have mentioned even other family members, since three of Sancia's four brothers, all of whom would have been groomed for royal office, eventually renounced their rights to hold royal titles and duties in order to follow a religious vocation.[81]

The fervor of faith in Sancia's family is all the more remarkable when one considers the strong military training and war culture which were central to medieval royalty. Sancia was, after all, the granddaughter of James of Aragon, known as "The Conqueror," and the daughter of James I, King of Majorca. The primary function of royalty was to acquire and preserve power through territory. While negotiation and diplomacy were sometimes used as tactics to achieve royal goals, warfare was a more common one. Therefore, Sancia and her brothers grew up within an environment of constant hostility or preparation for hostility. The pervasive Franciscan influence is noteworthy, and is likely directly attributable primarily to Sancia's mother, Sclaramonda.

---

[80] Musto, "Queen Sancia of Naples (1286-1345)," 208.
[81] Musto, "Queen Sancia of Naples (1286-1345)," 182.

As a royal princess, Sancia would have been reared with the expectation of marriage to another royal and would have been expected to bear children who would be heirs to the royal patrimony. Marriage was a political treaty binding two families – and in Sancia's case, two dynasties – together for a strategic alliance. Sancia's own marriage bound the Majorcan royal family to the House of Anjou, when she wed Robert, the third son of Charles II of Anjou in 1304. Strategically, the marriage was intended to form a powerful alliance that would affect much of the northern Mediterranean: the Italian peninsula, parts of southern France, and even stretches of Eastern Europe. Had children been born of this union, the Angevin claims to this vast territory would have continued throughout the fourteenth century. But Robert and Sancia were childless. The only legitimate heir born to Robert was with his first wife, Violante, who had died in 1302. The child born from this marriage, Charles, subsequently Duke of Calabria, died as a young man in 1328. Much has been written about the sterile marriage of Robert and Sancia, with many biographers pointing fingers of blame at Sancia for her overly zealous piety that cultivated in her a nun-like attitude toward conjugal relations.[82] While such interpretations of their childless marriage remain speculation, it is clear that Sancia took her faith seriously and felt she had a particular vocation to fill that did not involve bearing children.

Sancia gives notice of her strongly Franciscan-influenced vocation in a letter she wrote in 1334 to the Franciscan Chapter General meeting in Assisi and presents her royal office as integral to her religious call. In that letter she maps out her affiliation to the Franciscan Order through Robert's family:

---

[82] This kind of judgment is leveled in older scholarship. For example, see Welbore St. Clair Baddeley, *Robert the Wise and His Heirs* (London, 1897), esp. 162-63. More recent scholars have tended to opt for a more generous interpretation of the queen's religious convictions. In addition to Musto, "Queen Sancia of Naples (1286-1345)," see Caroline Bruzelius, *The Stones of Naples. Church Building in Angevin Italy, 1266-1343* (New Haven: Yale University Press, 2004), esp. chapter four.

He [God] also caused me to have a husband the most illustrious lord, my lord Robert, king of Jerusalem and Sicily, who was the son of Lady Marie, the well-remembered queen of these realms and of Hungary. She was also the true daughter of blessed Francis and bore a son, blessed Louis, who refused and renounced royal power for the love of Jesus Christ and became a Friar Minor. I also firmly believe that God and blessed Francis ordained that my lord – who was the third brother – would be king and would have all the virtues that were proper to him and more wisdom and knowledge than have been known of any prince of the world since the time of Solomon; and this knowledge he gathered from the friars of the order so that he – and I with him – might defend the order of blessed Francis.[83]

Through her marriage to Robert of the House of Anjou, Sancia found even more ancestral ties to the friars, most importantly through Robert's own brother, known as Louis of Toulouse, who was canonized as a saint in 1317 while Robert and Sancia ruled as monarchs of the kingdom of Naples.

From this position of ancestral bonds, Sancia positioned herself with Robert as effective protectors of the Franciscan order. It is only because of Louis's renunciation of his royal inheritance, that Robert, trained and educated as he was by friars, would become king, and in that office would be able to wield authority to protect the order. In this family lineage in which Sancia boasts of brothers who renounce their royal claims in order to become friars, she makes Robert's decision to accept the royal throne and rule the Angevin kingdom into an equally impressive addition to the families' Franciscan tree. While members of their families had renounced their royal office in order to fulfill their Franciscan call, Robert and Sancia would fulfill their own Franciscan vocations through their royal office.

---

[83] Musto, "Queen Sancia of Naples (1286-1345)," 208.

The couple did not initially share a vision of their royal office as a conduit for their Franciscan vocation. Instead, this vision developed over time and grew after the couple shared a fair amount of tension in their marriage. Having married in 1304, Sancia and Robert became monarchs in 1309. Theirs was an expansive kingdom that included the southern part of the Italian peninsula centered on the city of Naples, parts of southern France including Provence, and claims to the island of Sicily which Robert would forever try to regain.[84] In addition, Robert was papal vicar, and thereby was responsible for supporting papal interests especially as they played out on the Italian peninsula. Suffice it to say, Robert was preoccupied with things military and started his reign with determination to govern and expand his territorial claims.

His wife, however, did not share in these pursuits of power. Her interests are best revealed in the couple's foundation of the Poor Clare church of Corpus Christi, later known as Santa Chiara in Naples in 1310.[85] Although they both apparently placed the corner stone in a ceremonial foundation of the church, it seems more likely that Sancia was primarily responsible for the establishment of this monastery and church. The Poor Clares, as the female branch of the Franciscan world, quickly became the focus of the queen's spiritual and political attention. Some of Sancia's most memorable work was in founding religious houses dedicated to housing either established communities of Poor Clare sisters or new communities for reforming prostitutes. Her foundations were found throughout the couple's expansive kingdom including Naples, Marseilles and Aix.[86]

---

[84] The political claims of the Angevins also included Hungary and leadership of various city-states throughout the Italian peninsula. On the political life of the Angevins, see R. Caggese, *Roberto d'Angiò e i suoi tempi*, 2 vols. (Florence: Bemporad, 1922-30); E. Léonard, *Les angevins de naples*, (Paris: Presses universitaires de France, 1954).

[85] Luke Wadding, *Annales minorum*, VI, 1310, 178, xix, (Quaracchi, Ad Claras Aquas: Tipografia Barbèra, 1931), 200.

[86] On Sancia's architectural patronage, see Caroline Bruzelius, *The Stones of Naples,* esp. chapter 4 which specifically analyzes her role in founding the convent of Santa Chiara in Naples, which houses her tomb and that of her husband, Robert. For a catalogue of houses founded by San-

But Sancia's interest in the religious life was not limited to founding houses for other women. In 1312 Sancia requested and was granted permission to create something of a domestic monastery of her own at court. The pope allowed her to have a small group of Poor Clare nuns with her at all times.[87] Within five years the toll that this quasi-monastic life took on her marriage was clear. She wrote to Pope John XXII and requested a divorce from Robert so that she would be free to enter a convent. Once in 1316 and again on April 5, 1317 the pope wrote to her denying her request for the divorce. John XXII instead emphasized her conjugal duties as a wife. Sensing the cause of Sancia's spiritual yearnings included her husband's widely reputed philandering, the pope also wrote to Robert chastising him for not taking his marital vows seriously.[88]

These early frosty years eventually gave way to a different kind of marital and royal partnership in the 1320s. Robert was increasingly active as a theologian of sorts, preaching at a wide range of occasions and writing opinions on heated theological debates of the day.[89] In 1323 he submitted his own treatise on the nature of the poverty of Christ and the Apostles, as Pope John XXII had requested of all leading theologians at the papal curia and in leading universities. Although Robert's was not one of the opinions specifically requested, the king saw to it to send the work on to John XXII nevertheless.[90] As the papal vicar living in residence at the papal court in Avignon for a rather extended stay (1319-1324), Robert also inserted his opinions in theological and spiritual affairs by preaching specifically at the papal curia.

---

cia, see John Moorman, *Medieval Franciscan Houses*, Franciscan Institute Publications, History Series, no. 4 (St. Bonaventure, NY: The Franciscan Institute, 1983), 7, 236, 333, 538, 629-30.

[87] Wadding, VI, 1312, 203, xv, 227.

[88] Baddeley, *Robert the Wise*, 162-63.

[89] For an analysis of Robert's preaching role, see Darleen Pryds, *The King Embodies the Word: Robert d'Anjou and the Politics of Preaching*, (Leiden: Brill, 2000).

[90] For a further discussion of Robert's role as theological advisor to John XXII, see esp. ch. 5 of Pryds, *The King Embodies the Word*.

While contemporaries (and modern scholars) expressed annoyance at the king's theological activities, Robert expanded them upon a personal tragedy in his life. In 1328 his only son and direct heir, Charles, Duke of Calabria, suddenly and unexpectedly died. Some have conjectured that the death of his son caused Robert to sink into a spiritual crisis, since one can date from this point Robert's increasing focus on preaching and theological writing, and his particular concern for the Franciscan family in his kingdom. By 1335 the king had expanded the range of religious duties he took on, when he officially visited the religious houses of his kingdom, preaching at over twenty churches in six months.[91]

At times Robert's passion in sharing of Franciscan life proved to be overly exuberant, as when he was briefly excommunicated for bringing nobles into the convent of Corpus Christi, the convent of Poor Clare sisters that he founded with Sancia.[92] While he had sought official permission to enter the convent with twelve companions on the occasion of an anniversary associated with his own sainted brother, Louis of Toulouse, the crowd that actually gathered that day was larger, and some of the king's companions refused to listen to his sermon from behind the grate that enclosed the nuns. Robert allowed them to enter, preached the sermon, and immediately felt the compunction to ask forgiveness for his sin of bringing in secular elements into the convent. In a classic case of "It is better to ask forgiveness than permission," the king reported his misdeed and endured the penalty of brief excommunication.

While Robert's piety may never have reached the depths of his wife's, the direction he took with his royal office increasingly mirrored the pious course she had taken as queen from the beginning of her reign, so that one can see a spiritual and royal partnership forged from the 1320s until the king's death in 1343. It was during these years that the couple, spearheaded by Sancia's personal religious views and her fa-

---

[91] Pryds, *King Embodies the Word*, 119.

[92] Pope Benedict XII absolved Robert of his sentence of excommunication on January 10, 1338. Pryds, *King Embodies the Word*, 110.

milial fidelity, took bold steps that threatened the king's own alliance with Pope John XXII.

The couple's most extreme action evolved from their harboring a sect of Franciscans known as the Fraticelli in one of their royal castles in Naples. The Fraticelli fiercely embraced the ideal of poverty by imitating Francis's own literal interpretation of the ideal. Outspokenly critical, however, of how the rest of the Franciscan Order had developed and how most friars lived out this ideal, the Fraticelli rather self-righteously claimed to be the only legitimate followers of Francis. It was this strict idealism that attracted Sancia, perhaps because she was herself constantly accommodating her ideals to the royal culture in which she lived. Sancia's personal attraction to the Fraticelli was compounded by the fact that her brother, Philip of Majorca, was a leader of the group in Naples. Sancia and Robert gave shelter and protection to this group, and earned the ire of Pope John XXII for their support.[93]

This episode illustrates the couple's shared conviction that their role as monarchs included cultivating religious life along traditions they supported despite disciplinary action they faced as a result. It also illustrates the queen's own interest in supporting forms of religious life that she admired but found outside the realm of possibility for her own vocational call.

Sancia was finally able to live out her monastic call once Robert died in 1343. While there were some remaining royal functions for her to fulfill in the early months of transition for her step-granddaughter to take the throne, Sancia very quickly transitioned into a full-fledged nun. For the final year and a half of her life, Sancia lived quietly as a Poor Clare nun and was buried upon her death in 1345 in full habit.

---

[93] The Angevin interest in the Fraticelli is discussed in Decima Douie, *The Nature and Effect of the Heresy of the Fraticelli* (Manchester: University Press, 1932).

CONCLUSION

Sancia's intense attraction to the Franciscan ideal of apostolic poverty made her – to use a cliché – a fish out of water. Her life was one of constant accommodation and adaptation of her true vocation to the circumstances in which she found herself. Surrounded by the trappings of royal office, she transformed her personal monastic vocation into a life dedicated to using her royal office to shape religious life in her kingdom. She couldn't get what she wanted, so she did what she could.

While the details may differ, this tension between a life desired and a life experienced is something many lay people with intense experiences of faith have experienced throughout history. Sancia's life, then, can be used to explore how she managed to craft and sustain an authentic life of faith within her surroundings that would have easily pulled someone with a less developed piety away from a religious path.

STUDY QUESTIONS

1. In what ways did Sancia use her royal office to further Franciscan life in her kingdom?

2. List the number of ways Sancia affected Franciscan life, directly and indirectly in the Kingdom of Naples. What does this say about her view of spiritual authority?

REFLECTION QUESTIONS

1. Sancia found ways to accommodate her life to fit her religious vocation. In light of these accommodations, reflect on the following questions:

a. How do you respond to Sancia's approach to her married life?

b. Do you ever accommodate your religious vocation to fit your life?

c. How would your life change if you accommodated your life situation to fit your religious vocation?

d. Is accommodation necessary in the lay life?

2. Sancia spent much of her creative energy and resources to provide for those less fortunate in her kingdom. How do acts of charity fit into your vocation?

3. Sancia also spent much of her creative energy and resources in supporting religious life, especially the Poor Clares and Franciscans. How does supporting religious life – either of orders or your parish – fit into your vocation?

CONCLUSION

WOMEN OF THE STREETS:
THE FEARLESS FAITH
OF LAY FRANCISCAN WOMEN

The women studied in this volume all shared a passionate love of God. They expressed this passionate love through a Franciscan way of living in this world: they sought relationships. Through these relationships – with Christ, with the Virgin Mary, with contemporaries – they intensified their own spirituality and shared their intensifying faith fearlessly with others. Rose as a young child expressed her experience of the Divine with others by preaching in the streets; Angela offered counsel based on her own lived experience of suffering to those who sought advice; Margaret ministered to those who needed her medical and spiritual help; and Sancia used the privileged position of her royal office to aid those who were in need, when she probably would have preferred to have lived her life in prayer within the walls of a convent. Each of these women found a spiritual grounding through intense prayer-lives that blossomed into lives of service.

These laywomen who affiliated with the Franciscan tradition in the first century of the movement acquired religious education and attained recognition from their peers as significant spiritual leaders. Without formal education at a *studium* or university that contemporary friars pursued, these women carved out a special place for themselves in the intellectual tradition of the mendicant movement by living out the theological and spiritual precepts of the tradition. In keeping with Francis's own inspiration, these women embraced poverty first and foremost by embracing humility, cultivated through meditation on the suffering of Christ. The passion of Christ featured centrally in each of their stories even more than the figure of Francis. By contemplating Christ's suffering, each of these women achieved an internal strength and conviction that allowed them to fearlessly claim leadership roles in prayer and politics to their contemporaries. Each of them faced some amount of criticism, punishment, and ridicule, and yet their personal conviction could not be directed away from their vocations to love Christ and to share that love publicly. While Rose, Angela, Margaret, and Sancia each attained some position of leadership and authority in their respective lives, ultimately they shared one thing: they were women who experienced a love of Christ passionately and chose to share this love with others openly in the streets.

STUDY QUESTION

1. How are the faith lives of historical laywomen documented and preserved? How are the faith lives of present day women documented and preserved?

REFLECTION QUESTIONS

1. All of the women studied here are known through particular written sources that were recorded and preserved for reasons that could be labeled benignly as propaganda. They exist in order to reveal a certain view of these women.
   a. What sources exist that would tell future generations about your life of faith?
   b. What lessons could future lay people learn from these sources about a lay life of faith in the twenty-first century?

c. How might you consciously produce other sources to tell future generations about your life of faith? What would you say?

2. How do you share your experiences of God or your knowledge of Christ?

SELECT BIBLIOGRAPHY

Abate, Guiseppe. *S. Rosa di Viterbo, Terziana Francescana: Fonti Storiche della Vita e loro Revisione critica* (Rome: Editrice Miscellanea Francescana, 1952), orig. pub. in *Miscellanea Francescana* 52, fasc. 1-2 (Jan.-Jun., 1952): 112-278.

Bolzoni, Lina. *The Web of Images. Vernacular Preaching from its Origins to St. Bernardino of Siena.* Tran. Carole Preston and Lisa Chien. (Burlington, VT: Ashgate, 2004).

Bornstein, Daniel and Roberto Rusconi, eds. *Women and Religion in Medieval and Renaissance Italy.* Tran. Margery J. Schneider. (Chicago: University of Chicago Press, 1996).

Carmody, Maurice. *The Franciscan Story. St. Francis of Assisi and his Influence Since the 13th Century.* (London, Athena Press, 2008).

Cannon, Joanna and André Vauchez. *Margherita of Cortona and the Lorenzetti. Sienese Art and the Cult of a Holy Woman in Medieval Tuscany.* (University Park, Pennsylvania: Pennsylvania State University Press, 1999).

Carney, Margaret. *The First Franciscan Woman: Clare of Assisi and Her Form of Life.* (Quincy: Franciscan Press, 1993).

Coakley, John W. *Women, Men, and Spiritual Power. Female Saints and their Male Collaborators.* (New York: Columbia University Press, 2006).

D'Alatri, M. "Rosa di Viterbo: La santa a voce di popolo," *Italia Francescana* 44 (1969): 122-30.

Elliott, Dyan. *Proving Woman: Female Spirituality and Inquisitional Culture in the Later Middle Ages.* (Princeton: Princeton University Press, 2004).

Grundmann, Herbert. *Religious Movements in the Middle Ages.* Tran. Steven Rowan. (Notre Dame: University of Notre Dame Press, 1995).

Iozzelli, Fortunato, ed. *Iunctae Bevegnatis. Legenda de Vita et Miraculis Beatae Margaritae de Cortona,* Bibliotheca franciscana ascetica medii aevi, 13 (Grottaferrata: Editiones Collegii S. Bonaventurae ad Claras Aquas, 1997).

Knox, Lezlie. *Creating Clare of Assisi. Female Franciscan Identities in Later Medieval Italy.* (Leiden: Brill, 2008).

———— "'The True Daughters of Francis and Clare:' The Formation of The Order of Saint Clare in Late Medieval Italy," Ph.D. Dissertation, University of Notre Dame, 1999.

Lachance, Paul. Ed. and tran. *Angela of Foligno. Complete Works.* (New York: Paulist Press, 1993).

———— Ed. and Tran. *Angela of Foligno. Passionate Mystic of the Double Abyss.* (Hyde Park, NY: New City Press, 2006).

Makowski, Elizabeth. *"A Pernicious Sort of Woman": Quasi-Religious Women and Canon Lawyers in the Later Middle*

Ages. Studies in Medieval and Early Modern Canon Law, vol. 6. (Washington, DC: Catholic University of America, 2005)

Meany, Mary Walsh, "Angela of Foligno: A Eucharistic Model of Lay Sanctity," in *Lay Sanctity, Medieval and Modern. A Search for Models*. Ed. Ann Astell. (Notre Dame: University of Notre Dame Press, 2000), 61-75.

Merlo, Grado. *In the Name of Saint Francis. History of the Friars Minor and Franciscanism until the 16ᵗʰ Century*. Tran. Raphael Bonanno, ed. Robert Karris. (St. Bonaventure, NY: Franciscan Institute, 2009).

Meersemann, G. *Ordo Penitentialis. Confraternite e pietà dei laici nel Medioevo*. (Rome: Herder, 1977).

Mooney, Catherine. *"Gendered Voices." Medieval Saints and their Interpreters*. (Philadelphia: University of Pennsylvania Press, 1999).

Musto, Ronald. "Queen Sancia of Naples (1286-1345) and the Spiritual Franciscans," in *Women of the Medieval World. Essays in Honor of John H. Mundy*. Ed. Julius Kirschner and Suzanne Wemple. (Oxford: Basil Blackwell, 1985), 179-214.

Peterson, Ingrid. *Clare of Assisi A Biographical Study*. (Quincy: Franciscan Press, 1993).

Piacentini, Ernesto. *Il Libro dei miracoli di Santa Rosa di Viterbo*. (Viterbo: Basilica di Francesco alla Rocca, 1991).

Pryds, Darleen. "Following Francis: Laywomen and the Scandalous Call to be Franciscan," *Listening* 41.2 (2006): 85-95.

———— "Preaching Women: The Tradition of Mendicant Women" in *Franciscan Evangelization: Striving to Preach the Gospel*. Washington Theological Union Symposium Papers 7 (St. Bonaventure, NY: Franciscan Institute, 2008), 55-77.

———— "Proclaiming Sanctity through Proscribed Acts: The Case of Rose of Viterbo," in *Women Preachers and Prophets through Two Millennia*. Ed. Beverly Kienzle and Pamela Walker. (Berkeley: University of California Press, 1998), 159-72.

Schlager, Bernard, "Foundress of the Franciscan Life: Umiliani Cerchi and Margaret of Cortona, *Viator* 29 (1998): 141-66.

Short, William. *Poverty and Joy. The Franciscan Tradition*. (Maryknoll, NY: Orbis, 1999).

Vacca, Anna Maria. *La menta e la Croce*. (Rome: Bulzoni, 1982).

Vauchez, André. *The Laity in the Middle Ages. Religious Beliefs and Devotional Practices*. Tran. Margery Schneider, ed. Daniel Bornstein. (Notre Dame: University of Notre Dame Press, 1993).

———— "Saints admirables et saints imitables: les fonctions de l'hagiographie ont-elles changé aux derniers siècles du Moyen Age." *Les Fonctions des saints dans le monde occidental (IIIe-XIII siècle)*. Collection de l'École française de Rome, 149. (Rome: École Française de Rome, 1991), 161-72.

———— *Sainthood in the Later Middle Ages*. Tran. Jean Birrell. (Cambridge: Cambridge University Press, 1997).

Weisenbeck, Joan and Marlene Weisenbeck. "Rose of Viterbo: Preacher and Reconciler," in *Clare of Assisi: A Medieval and Modern Woman. Clarefest Selected Papers*. Ed. Ingrid Peterson. Clare Centenary Series, vol. 8. (St. Bonaventure, NY: The Franciscan Institute, 1996), 145-55.

Wiethaus, Ulrike, ed. *Maps of Flesh and Light. The Religious Experience of Medieval Women Mystics*. (Syracuse: Syracuse University Press, 1993).